MASTERING DATA STRUCTURES AND ALGORITHMS WITH PYTHON

A Complete Guide to Understanding and Implementing Key Data Structures and Algorithms for Software Development and Problem Solving

Author: ROGERS ISAACSON

Co Author: Katarina Jurić

1ST EDITION

TABLE OF CONTENTS

ABOUT THE AUTHORS!

Rogers Isaacson (Author)

Rogers Isaacson is a seasoned expert in **tech and programming**, with extensive experience in software architecture, development, and innovation. Over the years, he has worked with a wide range of technologies, providing cutting-edge solutions to global tech companies. Rogers is known for his ability to simplify complex concepts, making them accessible for developers of all skill levels. His passion for coding, combined with a deep understanding of emerging tech trends, has made him a sought-after mentor and thought leader in the tech community.

Katarina Jurić (Co-Author)

Katarina Jurić is a talented and innovative writer who brings a unique perspective to every tech project she collaborates on. Known for her collaborative spirit, Katarina enhances the content with her in-depth research and creative approach to complex tech topics. Her writing style blends technical precision with engaging storytelling, ensuring that every piece resonates with readers while providing valuable insights. With a keen understanding of emerging trends and practical tech applications, Katarina works tirelessly to produce content that is not only technically accurate but also enjoyable to read. Her ability to simplify even the most complex tech concepts has made her a valuable contributor to the tech writing niche.

CHAPTER 1:
INTRODUCTION TO
DATA STRUCTURES AND
ALGORITHMS

1. Introduction

I n the ever-evolving landscape of software development, the ability to efficiently manage and manipulate data is paramount. At the heart of this capability lie two fundamental pillars: Data Structures and Algorithms. Understanding these concepts is not just beneficial; it's essential for anyone aspiring to excel in the field of programming, whether you're a beginner taking your first steps or an intermediate learner aiming to deepen your expertise.

Why Should You Care About Data Structures and Algorithms?

Imagine attempting to organize a vast library without any system. Finding a specific book would be akin to searching for a needle in a haystack. Similarly, in software development, inefficient data handling can lead to sluggish applications, increased resource consumption, and a poor user experience. Data Structures and Algorithms (DS&A) provide the blueprint for organizing, managing, and processing data efficiently, ensuring that software applications are both robust and performant.

Key Concepts and Terminology

Before diving deeper, let's clarify some essential terms:

- Data Structure: A specialized format for organizing, processing, and storing data. Examples include arrays, linked lists, stacks, queues, trees, and graphs.

- Algorithm: A step-by-step procedure or formula for solving a problem. Algorithms dictate how data is processed within data structures.

- Big O Notation: A mathematical notation used to describe the performance or complexity of an algorithm, particularly its time and space requirements.

Setting the Tone

Embarking on the journey to master DS&A can seem daunting, but with the right guidance and practical approach, it becomes an engaging and rewarding experience. This chapter serves as your gateway into the world of data structures and algorithms, providing a solid foundation that will empower you to tackle complex programming challenges with confidence.

2. Core Concepts and Theory

Understanding Data Structures and Algorithms is akin to learning the grammar and vocabulary of a new language. They form the syntax and semantics through which software communicates and operates. This section delves into the core concepts, demystifying the theories behind DS&A and illustrating their real-world applications.

2.1. What Are Data Structures?

At their core, data structures are ways of organizing and storing data to enable efficient access and modification. The choice of data structure directly impacts the performance of algorithms and, by extension, the overall efficiency of software applications.

Types of Data Structures:

1. Primitive Data Structures: These are the basic building blocks, such as integers, floats, characters, and booleans.

2. Non-Primitive Data Structures: These are more complex and include:

   o Linear Data Structures: Arrays, Lists, Stacks, Queues.

   o Non-Linear Data Structures: Trees, Graphs.

Real-World Analogy:

Think of data structures as different types of containers:

- Array: Like a bookshelf where each slot holds a book, and each book is accessible by its position.

- Linked List: Imagine a chain of paperclips where each clip knows only about the next one.

- Stack: A stack of plates; you add and remove plates from the top.

- Queue: People standing in line; the first person to join the queue is the first to be served.

- Tree: An organizational chart showing hierarchical relationships.

- Graph: A map of cities connected by roads, representing relationships between different entities.

2.2. What Are Algorithms?

Algorithms are precise instructions or procedures for performing tasks or solving problems. They are the recipes that dictate how data is processed within data structures.

Key Characteristics of Algorithms:

- Finite: They must terminate after a finite number of steps.

- Definite: Each step must be clearly and unambiguously defined.

- Input and Output: They have zero or more inputs and produce at least one output.

- Effectiveness: Each step must be basic enough to be carried out, in principle, by a person using only pencil and paper.

Common Algorithm Categories:

1. Sorting Algorithms: Organize data in a particular order (e.g., Bubble Sort, Merge Sort, Quick Sort).

2. Searching Algorithms: Retrieve information stored within data structures (e.g., Linear Search, Binary Search).

3. Recursive Algorithms: Solve problems by breaking them down into smaller, more manageable sub-problems.

4. Dynamic Programming: Optimize algorithms by storing the results of expensive function calls and reusing them when the same inputs occur again.

Real-World Example:

Consider planning a road trip. An algorithm would outline the steps you take: planning your route (sorting), finding the nearest gas stations (searching), and deciding on rest stops (optimization).

2.3. Importance of DS&A in Software Development

Data Structures and Algorithms are foundational to writing efficient and effective code. Here's why they matter:

- Performance Optimization: Efficient algorithms reduce the time and resources required to perform tasks, leading to faster and more responsive applications.

- Scalability: Properly chosen data structures ensure that applications can handle increasing amounts of data without a significant drop in performance.

- Problem-Solving: DS&A provide a toolkit for tackling complex programming challenges, enabling developers to devise optimal solutions.

- Technical Interviews: Mastery of DS&A is often a prerequisite for technical job interviews, as they demonstrate a candidate's problem-solving abilities and coding proficiency.

Case Study: Google's Search Engine

Google's search algorithm is a prime example of how DS&A drive real-world applications. It utilizes complex data structures like inverted indexes and algorithms for ranking pages to deliver relevant search results in milliseconds, handling billions of queries daily.

2.4. Big O Notation: Measuring Algorithm Efficiency

Big O Notation is a mathematical concept used to describe the efficiency of algorithms, particularly in terms of time and space complexity.

Understanding Big O:

- Time Complexity: Represents the amount of time an algorithm takes to complete as a function of the length of the input.

- Space Complexity: Represents the amount of memory an algorithm uses as a function of the length of the input.

Common Big O Classifications:

- **O(1): Constant time** - the operation doesn't depend on the input size.

- **O(log n): Logarithmic time** - increases logarithmically with the input size.

- **O(n): Linear time** - increases linearly with the input size.

- **O(n log n): Log-linear time** - increases faster than linear but slower than quadratic.

- **O(n²): Quadratic time** - increases proportionally to the square of the input size.

Practical Implications:

Choosing an algorithm with a lower Big O classification can significantly enhance performance, especially with large datasets. For instance, an O(n log n) sorting algorithm like Merge Sort outperforms an O(n²) algorithm like Bubble Sort as the number of elements increases.

3. Tools and Setup

Before diving into Data Structures and Algorithms, it's essential to set up your development environment. This section outlines the tools and platforms you'll need, providing step-by-step instructions to ensure a smooth setup process.

3.1. Required Tools and Platforms

1. **Python Programming Language:**

   o **Version:** Python 3.8 or higher is recommended for its modern features and improved performance.

   o **Installation:** Available for free from the official Python website.

2. **Integrated Development Environment (IDE) or Code Editor:**

   o **Options:**

      ▪ **Visual Studio Code (VS Code):** A free, versatile code editor with extensive extensions.

- **PyCharm:** A powerful IDE specifically designed for Python, available in both free and paid versions.

- **Jupyter Notebook:** Ideal for interactive coding and visualization, especially useful for data science projects.

3. **Version Control System:**

   o **Git:** A distributed version control system to track changes and collaborate on code.

   o **Installation:** Download from the official Git website.

   o **Optional:** GitHub or GitLab accounts for remote repository hosting.

4. **Python Libraries:**

   o **Standard Libraries:** Python comes with a rich set of built-in libraries that support various data structures and algorithms.

   o **Additional Libraries:** Depending on the projects, libraries like numpy, pandas, and matplotlib might be useful.

3.2. Step-by-Step Setup Guide

Step 1: Installing Python

1. **Download Python:**

   o Navigate to the Python Downloads page.

   o Select the appropriate installer for your operating system (Windows, macOS, Linux).

2. **Run the Installer:**

   o Execute the downloaded installer.

   o **Important:** Check the box that says "Add Python to PATH" to ensure that Python is accessible from the command line.

3. **Verify Installation:**

   o Open your terminal or command prompt.

   o Type python --version and press Enter.

   o You should see the installed Python version number.

Step 2: Installing an IDE or Code Editor

1. **Visual Studio Code:**

   o **Visit the <u>VS Code website</u>.**

   o **Download and install the version compatible with your OS.**

   o **Extensions to Install:**

     ▪ **Python Extension: Provides IntelliSense, linting, debugging, and more.**

     ▪ **GitLens: Enhances Git capabilities within VS Code.**

2. **PyCharm:**

   o **Go to the <u>PyCharm Downloads</u> page.**

   o **Choose between the Community (free) or Professional (paid) editions.**

   o **Install following the on-screen instructions.**

3. **Jupyter Notebook:**

   o **Install via pip:**

bash

pip install notebook

   o **Launch by typing jupyter notebook in your terminal.**

Step 3: Installing Git

1. **Download Git:**

   o **Access the <u>Git Downloads</u> page.**

   o **Choose the installer for your OS.**

2. **Run the Installer:**

   o **Follow the installation prompts, accepting default settings is generally recommended.**

3. **Configure Git:**

       o   Open your terminal and set your username and email:

bash

```
git config --global user.name "Your Name"
git config --global user.email "youremail@example.com"
```

Step 4: Installing Python Libraries

1. **Using pip:**

       o   Open your terminal.

       o   Install libraries as needed. For example:

bash

```
pip install numpy pandas matplotlib
```

2. **Verifying Installation:**

       o   In your Python environment, try importing the library:

python

```
import numpy
import pandas
import matplotlib
```

4. Hands-on Examples & Projects

Theory without practice can leave concepts abstract and challenging to grasp. This section bridges the gap between understanding and application, guiding you through practical examples and projects that reinforce the core concepts of Data Structures and Algorithms.

4.1. Project 1: Creating a Simple Dictionary Application

Objective:

Build a basic dictionary application that allows users to add, search, and delete words along with their definitions. This project will utilize Python's built-in data structures to manage the data efficiently.

Key Concepts Covered:

- **Hash Tables:** Implementing the dictionary using Python's dict type.

- **User Input Handling:** Interacting with users via the command line.

- **Basic CRUD Operations:** Creating, Reading, Updating, and Deleting entries.

Step-by-Step Implementation:

Step 1: Setting Up the Project Structure

Create a new Python file named dictionary_app.py.

Step 2: Defining the Dictionary Data Structure

python

```
# dictionary_app.py


# Initialize an empty dictionary to store words and their definitions

dictionary = {}
```

Step 3: Implementing CRUD Operations

python

```
def add_word(word, definition):
    if word in dictionary:
        print(f"The word '{word}' already exists in the dictionary.")
    else:
        dictionary[word] = definition
        print(f"Word '{word}' added successfully.")
```

```python
def search_word(word):

    definition = dictionary.get(word)

    if definition:

        print(f"{word}: {definition}")

    else:

        print(f"The word '{word}' was not found in the dictionary.")


def delete_word(word):

    if word in dictionary:

        del dictionary[word]

        print(f"Word '{word}' deleted successfully.")

    else:

        print(f"The word '{word}' does not exist in the dictionary.")
```

Step 4: Creating the User Interface

python

```python
def display_menu():

    print("\nDictionary Application")

    print("1. Add a new word")

    print("2. Search for a word")

    print("3. Delete a word")

    print("4. Exit")


def main():

    while True:
```

```python
    display_menu()

    choice = input("Enter your choice (1-4): ")


    if choice == '1':

        word = input("Enter the word: ").strip().lower()

        definition = input("Enter the definition: ").strip()

        add_word(word, definition)

    elif choice == '2':

        word = input("Enter the word to search: ").strip().lower()

        search_word(word)

    elif choice == '3':

        word = input("Enter the word to delete: ").strip().lower()

        delete_word(word)

    elif choice == '4':

        print("Exiting the Dictionary Application. Goodbye!")

        break

    else:

        print("Invalid choice. Please try again.")


if __name__ == "__main__":

    main()
```

Step 5: Running the Application

1. Open your terminal or command prompt.

2. Navigate to the directory containing dictionary_app.py.

3. Execute the script:

bash

python dictionary_app.py

    4.   Interact with the application by adding, searching, and deleting words.

Sample Interaction:

mathematica

Dictionary Application

1. Add a new word

2. Search for a word

3. Delete a word

4. Exit

Enter your choice (1-4): 1

Enter the word: Python

Enter the definition: A high-level programming language.

Word 'python' added successfully.

Dictionary Application

1. Add a new word

2. Search for a word

3. Delete a word

4. Exit

Enter your choice (1-4): 2

Enter the word to search: python

python: A high-level programming language.

4.2. Project 2: Designing a Browser History Manager

Objective:

Develop a browser history manager that simulates the back and forward navigation features of a web browser. This project will utilize stacks to manage the history of visited pages.

Key Concepts Covered:

- **Stacks:** Implementing back and forward navigation using stack data structures.

- **Class Design:** Creating classes to encapsulate the functionality.

- **Error Handling:** Managing edge cases where navigation isn't possible.

Step-by-Step Implementation:

Step 1: Understanding the Stack Data Structure

A stack operates on the Last-In-First-Out (LIFO) principle. We'll use two stacks:

- **Back Stack:** Keeps track of pages visited before the current page.

- **Forward Stack:** Keeps track of pages navigated forward to.

Step 2: Implementing the BrowserHistory Class

python

```
# browser_history.py


class BrowserHistory:
    def __init__(self, homepage):
        self.back_stack = []
        self.forward_stack = []
        self.current_page = homepage
        print(f"Browser initialized with homepage: {self.current_page}")
```

```python
def visit(self, url):

    self.back_stack.append(self.current_page)

    self.current_page = url

    self.forward_stack.clear()

    print(f"Visited: {self.current_page}")


def back(self, steps=1):

    while steps > 0 and self.back_stack:

        self.forward_stack.append(self.current_page)

        self.current_page = self.back_stack.pop()

        steps -= 1

        print(f"Moved back to: {self.current_page}")

    if steps > 0:

        print("No more pages to go back to.")


def forward(self, steps=1):

    while steps > 0 and self.forward_stack:

        self.back_stack.append(self.current_page)

        self.current_page = self.forward_stack.pop()

        steps -= 1

        print(f"Moved forward to: {self.current_page}")

    if steps > 0:

        print("No more pages to go forward to.")


def current(self):
```

```python
        print(f"Current page: {self.current_page}")

        return self.current_page
```

Step 3: Creating the User Interface

python

```python
def display_menu():
    print("\nBrowser History Manager")
    print("1. Visit a new page")
    print("2. Go back")
    print("3. Go forward")
    print("4. Show current page")
    print("5. Exit")


def main():
    homepage = input("Enter the homepage URL: ").strip()
    browser = BrowserHistory(homepage)

    while True:
        display_menu()
        choice = input("Enter your choice (1-5): ")

        if choice == '1':
            url = input("Enter the URL to visit: ").strip()
            browser.visit(url)
        elif choice == '2':
            steps = int(input("Enter the number of steps to go back: ").strip())
```

```python
            browser.back(steps)
        elif choice == '3':
            steps = int(input("Enter the number of steps to go forward: ").strip())
            browser.forward(steps)
        elif choice == '4':
            browser.current()
        elif choice == '5':
            print("Exiting Browser History Manager. Goodbye!")
            break
        else:
            print("Invalid choice. Please try again.")


if __name__ == "__main__":
    main()
```

Step 4: Running the Browser History Manager

1. Open your terminal.

2. Navigate to the directory containing browser_history.py.

3. Run the script:

bash

```
python browser_history.py
```

4. Follow the prompts to interact with the browser history manager.

Sample Interaction:

mathematica

Enter the homepage URL: https://www.example.com

Browser initialized with homepage: https://www.example.com

Browser History Manager

1. Visit a new page

2. Go back

3. Go forward

4. Show current page

5. Exit

Enter your choice (1-5): 1

Enter the URL to visit: https://www.openai.com

Visited: https://www.openai.com

Browser History Manager

1. Visit a new page

2. Go back

3. Go forward

4. Show current page

5. Exit

Enter your choice (1-5): 2

Enter the number of steps to go back: 1

Moved back to: https://www.example.com

4.3. Project 3: Building a File System Explorer

Objective:

Create a simple file system explorer that allows users to navigate through directories, list files, and perform basic operations. This project utilizes tree data structures to represent the hierarchical nature of file systems.

Key Concepts Covered:

- Trees: Implementing a file system hierarchy using tree structures.

- Recursion: Navigating directories recursively.

- File Operations: Listing and managing files and directories.

Step-by-Step Implementation:

Step 1: Understanding the Tree Data Structure

A tree consists of nodes connected by edges, with a single root node. Each node can have multiple child nodes, representing directories and subdirectories.

Step 2: Implementing the FileSystemNode Class

python

```python
# file_system_explorer.py


class FileSystemNode:
    def __init__(self, name, is_file=False):
        self.name = name
        self.is_file = is_file
        self.children = []  # Only directories will have children


    def add_child(self, child_node):
        if not self.is_file:
            self.children.append(child_node)
        else:
            print("Cannot add child to a file.")
```

```python
def list_children(self):
    if self.is_file:
        print(f"{self.name} is a file and has no children.")
    else:
        for child in self.children:
            type_indicator = "File" if child.is_file else "Directory"
            print(f"{child.name} - {type_indicator}")
```

Step 3: Creating the File System Structure

python

```python
def create_sample_file_system():
    root = FileSystemNode("root")

    # Adding directories
    documents = FileSystemNode("Documents")
    photos = FileSystemNode("Photos")
    music = FileSystemNode("Music")
    root.add_child(documents)
    root.add_child(photos)
    root.add_child(music)

    # Adding files to Documents
    resume = FileSystemNode("Resume.docx", is_file=True)
    project = FileSystemNode("Project", is_file=False)
    documents.add_child(resume)
```

```python
documents.add_child(project)


# Adding files to Project
code = FileSystemNode("code.py", is_file=True)
design = FileSystemNode("design.png", is_file=True)
project.add_child(code)
project.add_child(design)


# Adding files to Photos
vacation = FileSystemNode("Vacation", is_file=False)
photos.add_child(vacation)
beach = FileSystemNode("beach.jpg", is_file=True)
vacation.add_child(beach)


# Adding files to Music
song = FileSystemNode("song.mp3", is_file=True)
music.add_child(song)


return root
```

Step 4: Implementing Navigation and Operations

python

```python
def display_menu():
    print("\nFile System Explorer")
    print("1. List current directory")
    print("2. Navigate to a directory")
```

```python
        print("3. Go back to parent directory")

        print("4. Exit")


def list_current_directory(current_node):

    print(f"\nContents of '{current_node.name}':")

    current_node.list_children()


def navigate_to_directory(current_node, path):

    parts = path.strip().split("/")

    node = current_node

    for part in parts:

        found = False

        for child in node.children:

            if child.name.lower() == part.lower() and not child.is_file:

                node = child

                found = True

                break

        if not found:

            print(f"Directory '{part}' not found.")

            return current_node

    print(f"Navigated to '{node.name}'")

    return node


def main():

    root = create_sample_file_system()

    current_node = root
```

```python
    history = []

    while True:
        display_menu()
        choice = input("Enter your choice (1-4): ")

        if choice == '1':
            list_current_directory(current_node)
        elif choice == '2':
            path = input("Enter the directory path to navigate (e.g., Documents/Project): ").strip()
            if path:
                history.append(current_node)
                current_node = navigate_to_directory(current_node, path)
        elif choice == '3':
            if history:
                current_node = history.pop()
                print(f"Returned to '{current_node.name}'")
            else:
                print("Already at the root directory.")
        elif choice == '4':
            print("Exiting File System Explorer. Goodbye!")
            break
        else:
            print("Invalid choice. Please try again.")


if __name__ == "__main__":
```

```
main()
```

Step 5: Running the File System Explorer

1. Open your terminal.

2. Navigate to the directory containing file_system_explorer.py.

3. Run the script:

bash

```
python file_system_explorer.py
```

4. Use the menu to navigate through directories, list contents, and perform operations.

Sample Interaction:

mathematica

File System Explorer

1. List current directory

2. Navigate to a directory

3. Go back to parent directory

4. Exit

Enter your choice (1-4): 1

Contents of 'root':

Documents - Directory

Photos - Directory

Music - Directory

File System Explorer

1. List current directory

2. Navigate to a directory

3. Go back to parent directory

4. Exit

Enter your choice (1-4): 2

Enter the directory path to navigate (e.g., Documents/Project): Documents/Project

Navigated to 'Project'

File System Explorer

1. List current directory

2. Navigate to a directory

3. Go back to parent directory

4. Exit

Enter your choice (1-4): 1

Contents of 'Project':

code.py - File

design.png - File

5. Advanced Techniques & Optimization

Having grasped the fundamentals, it's time to delve into advanced techniques that enhance the efficiency and scalability of your data structures and algorithms. This section explores optimization strategies, best practices, and advanced concepts that will elevate your programming prowess.

5.1. Heaps and Priority Queues

Understanding Heaps:

A heap is a specialized tree-based data structure that satisfies the heap property:

- **Max Heap:** The value of each node is greater than or equal to the values of its children.

- **Min Heap:** The value of each node is less than or equal to the values of its children.

Applications:

- **Priority Queues:** Efficiently manage elements based on priority.

- **Heap Sort:** An efficient comparison-based sorting algorithm.

- **Graph Algorithms:** Used in algorithms like Dijkstra's shortest path.

Implementing a Min Heap in Python:

Python's heapq module provides an efficient implementation of the heap queue algorithm, also known as the priority queue algorithm.

python

```python
import heapq


class MinHeap:
    def __init__(self):
        self.heap = []


    def insert(self, item):
        heapq.heappush(self.heap, item)
        print(f"Inserted {item} into the heap.")


    def extract_min(self):
        if self.heap:
            min_item = heapq.heappop(self.heap)
```

```python
            print(f"Extracted min item: {min_item}")

            return min_item

        else:

            print("Heap is empty.")

            return None


    def peek_min(self):

        if self.heap:

            print(f"Current min item: {self.heap[0]}")

            return self.heap[0]

        else:

            print("Heap is empty.")

            return None


    def display_heap(self):

        print(f"Heap contents: {self.heap}")
```

Usage Example:

python

```python
def heap_example():

    heap = MinHeap()

    heap.insert(10)

    heap.insert(4)

    heap.insert(15)

    heap.insert(20)

    heap.display_heap()
```

```
    heap.peek_min()

    heap.extract_min()

    heap.display_heap()


if __name__ == "__main__":

    heap_example()
```

Output:

sql

Inserted 10 into the heap.

Inserted 4 into the heap.

Inserted 15 into the heap.

Inserted 20 into the heap.

Heap contents: [4, 10, 15, 20]

Current min item: 4

Extracted min item: 4

Heap contents: [10, 20, 15]

Optimization Tips:

- **Lazy Deletion:** Instead of removing elements immediately, mark them for deletion and remove them when they reach the top of the heap. This can improve performance in certain scenarios.

- **Custom Comparisons:** Modify the heap to handle complex data types by defining custom comparison methods or using tuples where the first element dictates the priority.

5.2. Tries and Suffix Trees

Understanding Tries:

A trie, also known as a prefix tree, is a tree-like data structure used to store associative data structures, typically strings. It's highly efficient for tasks like autocomplete and spell checking.

Applications:

- Autocomplete Systems: Quickly suggest words based on prefixes.

- Spell Checkers: Efficiently verify the existence of words.

- IP Routing: Optimizing longest prefix matching.

Implementing a Simple Trie in Python:

python

```python
class TrieNode:
    def __init__(self):
        self.children = {}
        self.is_end_of_word = False


class Trie:
    def __init__(self):
        self.root = TrieNode()


    def insert(self, word):
        node = self.root
        for char in word.lower():
            if char not in node.children:
                node.children[char] = TrieNode()
            node = node.children[char]
        node.is_end_of_word = True
        print(f"Inserted '{word}' into the trie.")
```

```python
def search(self, word):
    node = self.root
    for char in word.lower():
        if char not in node.children:
            print(f"'{word}' not found in the trie.")
            return False
        node = node.children[char]
    if node.is_end_of_word:
        print(f"'{word}' found in the trie.")
        return True
    else:
        print(f"'{word}' is a prefix in the trie but not a complete word.")
        return False


def starts_with(self, prefix):
    node = self.root
    for char in prefix.lower():
        if char not in node.children:
            print(f"No words start with '{prefix}'.")
            return False
        node = node.children[char]
    print(f"There are words that start with '{prefix}'.")
    return True
```

Usage Example:

python

```python
def trie_example():

    trie = Trie()

    words = ["hello", "helium", "helicopter", "help", "hero"]

    for word in words:

        trie.insert(word)


    trie.search("hello")

    trie.search("helix")

    trie.starts_with("hel")

    trie.starts_with("hex")


if __name__ == "__main__":

    trie_example()
```

Output:

sql

Inserted 'hello' into the trie.

Inserted 'helium' into the trie.

Inserted 'helicopter' into the trie.

Inserted 'help' into the trie.

Inserted 'hero' into the trie.

'hello' found in the trie.

'helix' not found in the trie.

There are words that start with 'hel'.

No words start with 'hex'.

Optimization Tips:

- **Space Optimization:** Use techniques like compressed tries or ternary search trees to reduce memory usage.

- **Lazy Initialization:** Initialize child nodes only when necessary to save space.

- **Parallelization:** Leverage concurrent processing for inserting and searching large datasets.

5.3. Algorithm Optimization and Big O Notation

Deep Dive into Big O:

Understanding the efficiency of algorithms is crucial for writing performant code. Big O Notation provides a high-level understanding of how an algorithm's runtime or space requirements grow relative to the input size.

Common Big O Classes Explained:

1. **O(1) - Constant Time:**

   o Operations that take the same amount of time regardless of input size.

   o Example: Accessing an element in an array by index.

2. **O(log n) - Logarithmic Time:**

   o Operations that reduce the problem size with each step.

   o Example: Binary search in a sorted array.

3. **O(n) - Linear Time:**

   o Operations that scale linearly with input size.

   o Example: Iterating through all elements in a list.

4. **O(n log n) - Log-Linear Time:**

   o Common in efficient sorting algorithms.

   o Example: Merge Sort, Quick Sort.

5. **O(n²) - Quadratic Time:**

- o Operations with nested iterations over the input.

- o Example: Bubble Sort, Insertion Sort.

Practical Example: Comparing Sorting Algorithms

Let's compare Bubble Sort ($O(n^2)$) with Merge Sort ($O(n \log n)$) in terms of performance.

Bubble Sort Implementation:

python

```python
def bubble_sort(arr):
    n = len(arr)
    for i in range(n):
        for j in range(0, n-i-1):
            if arr[j] > arr[j+1]:
                arr[j], arr[j+1] = arr[j+1], arr[j]
    return arr
```

Merge Sort Implementation:

python

```python
def merge_sort(arr):
    if len(arr) > 1:
        mid = len(arr) // 2
        L = arr[:mid]
        R = arr[mid:]

        merge_sort(L)
        merge_sort(R)
```

```python
    i = j = k = 0

    # Merging the sorted halves
    while i < len(L) and j < len(R):
        if L[i] < R[j]:
            arr[k] = L[i]
            i += 1
        else:
            arr[k] = R[j]
            j += 1
        k += 1

    # Checking for any remaining elements
    while i < len(L):
        arr[k] = L[i]
        i += 1
        k += 1

    while j < len(R):
        arr[k] = R[j]
        j += 1
        k += 1
return arr
```

Performance Comparison:

python

```python
import time

import random


def performance_test():
    # Generate a list of random integers
    arr = random.sample(range(1, 10000), 1000)
    arr_ = arr.()


    # Time Bubble Sort
    start_time = time.time()
    bubble_sorted = bubble_sort(arr)
    bubble_time = time.time() - start_time
    print(f"Bubble Sort Time: {bubble_time:.6f} seconds")


    # Time Merge Sort
    start_time = time.time()
    merge_sorted = merge_sort(arr_)
    merge_time = time.time() - start_time
    print(f"Merge Sort Time: {merge_time:.6f} seconds")


if __name__ == "__main__":
    performance_test()
```

Sample Output:

mathematica

Bubble Sort Time: 0.456789 seconds

Merge Sort Time: 0.012345 seconds

Analysis:

As the output demonstrates, Merge Sort significantly outperforms Bubble Sort, especially as the input size grows. Understanding these differences allows developers to make informed decisions about which algorithms to implement based on the specific requirements and constraints of their projects.

Optimization Strategies:

- **Choosing the Right Algorithm:** Select algorithms that offer the best time and space complexity for your use case.

- **Data Structure Alignment:** Ensure that the chosen data structures complement the algorithm's requirements for optimal performance.

- **Code Profiling:** Use profiling tools to identify bottlenecks and optimize critical sections of your code.

5.4. Best Practices for Efficient Coding

1. **Avoid Premature Optimization:**

    o Focus on writing clear and correct code first. Optimize later based on profiling data.

2. **Leverage Built-in Data Structures and Libraries:**

    o Python's standard library is highly optimized. Utilize built-in functions and data types for better performance.

3. **Write Modular Code:**

    o Break down complex problems into smaller, manageable functions or classes. This enhances readability and maintainability.

4. **Use Recursion Wisely:**

    o While recursion can simplify code, excessive recursive calls can lead to stack overflow errors. Consider iterative solutions when appropriate.

5. **Understand Memory Management:**

    o Be mindful of how data structures consume memory, especially when dealing with large datasets.

6. Troubleshooting and Problem-Solving

Encountering challenges is an inevitable part of learning and implementing Data Structures and Algorithms. This section addresses common issues you might face, offering solutions and best practices to overcome them.

6.1. Common Challenges in DS&A

1. **Understanding Complex Concepts:**

   o **Issue:** Abstract theories can be hard to grasp without practical application.

   o **Solution:** Reinforce learning by implementing concepts through projects and visualizing data structures.

2. **Debugging Recursive Algorithms:**

   o **Issue:** Recursion can lead to confusing bugs and stack overflows.

   o **Solution:** Use debugging tools and step through recursive calls to understand the flow.

3. **Managing Large Codebases:**

   o **Issue:** Implementing multiple data structures can result in extensive and unwieldy code.

   o **Solution:** Adopt modular programming practices, using classes and functions to organize code logically.

4. **Optimizing Performance:**

   o **Issue:** Inefficient algorithms can cause performance bottlenecks.

   o **Solution:** Analyze time and space complexities, and choose more efficient algorithms or data structures as needed.

6.2. Troubleshooting Tips

Tip 1: Use Print Statements and Logging

Inserting print statements at critical points in your code can help trace the flow of execution and identify where things might be going wrong.

Example:

python

```python
def factorial(n):

    print(f"Calculating factorial of {n}")

    if n == 0:

        return 1

    else:

        result = n * factorial(n-1)

        print(f"factorial({n}) = {result}")

        return result
```

Tip 2: Leverage Debugging Tools

Most IDEs come with built-in debugging tools that allow you to set breakpoints, inspect variables, and step through code line by line.

Example in VS Code:

1. **Open browser_history.py in VS Code.**

2. **Click on the gutter next to the line number to set a breakpoint.**

3. **Run the debugger by pressing F5.**

4. **Use the debugger controls to step through the code and inspect variables.**

Tip 3: Validate Inputs and Handle Exceptions

Ensure that your code gracefully handles unexpected inputs and scenarios by validating inputs and using try-except blocks.

Example:

python

```python
def divide(a, b):
```

```python
    try:

        result = a / b

        print(f"Result of division: {result}")

        return result

    except ZeroDivisionError:

        print("Error: Cannot divide by zero.")

        return None


divide(10, 2)  # Valid division

divide(10, 0)  # Triggers exception handling
```

Output:

vbnet

Result of division: 5.0

Error: Cannot divide by zero.

Tip 4: Write Unit Tests

Implementing unit tests helps verify that individual components of your code work as intended.

Example Using unittest:

python

```python
import unittest


def add(a, b):

    return a + b


class TestMathFunctions(unittest.TestCase):
```

```python
    def test_add(self):

        self.assertEqual(add(2, 3), 5)

        self.assertEqual(add(-1, 1), 0)

        self.assertEqual(add(0, 0), 0)


if __name__ == "__main__":

    unittest.main()
```

Running the Tests:

bash

```bash
python test_math_functions.py
```

Output:

markdown

```
...

----------------------------------------------------------------

Ran 1 test in 0.000s


OK
```

6.3. Problem-Solving Strategies

1. **Break Down the Problem:**

    o   Divide complex problems into smaller, manageable parts. Tackle each
        part individually before integrating them.

2. **Pseudocode First:**

    o   Write pseudocode to outline the logic and flow of your algorithm
        before translating it into actual code.

3. **Visualize the Data Structures:**

- Drawing diagrams or using visualization tools can help you understand how data is organized and manipulated.

4. **Seek Patterns:**

- Identify patterns or similarities with problems you've previously solved. Reusing known solutions can save time and effort.

5. **Review and Refactor:**

- Regularly review your code for potential improvements. Refactoring can lead to more efficient and readable code.

Example: Solving the Fibonacci Sequence Problem

Problem: Write a function to compute the nth Fibonacci number.

Approach:

1. **Understand the Problem:**

- The Fibonacci sequence is defined as:
  - $F(0) = 0$
  - $F(1) = 1$
  - $F(n) = F(n-1) + F(n-2)$ for $n > 1$

2. **Choose a Strategy:**

- Recursive approach.
- Iterative approach.
- Dynamic programming (memoization).

3. **Implement the Solution:**

Recursive Implementation:

python

```python
def fibonacci_recursive(n):
    if n <= 0:
        return 0
```

```python
    elif n == 1:
        return 1
    else:
        return fibonacci_recursive(n-1) + fibonacci_recursive(n-2)
```

Iterative Implementation:

python

```python
def fibonacci_iterative(n):
    a, b = 0, 1
    for _ in range(n):
        a, b = b, a + b
    return a
```

Dynamic Programming Implementation:

python

```python
def fibonacci_memoization(n, memo={}):
    if n in memo:
        return memo[n]
    if n <= 0:
        memo[n] = 0
    elif n == 1:
        memo[n] = 1
    else:
        memo[n] = fibonacci_memoization(n-1, memo) + fibonacci_memoization(n-2, memo)
    return memo[n]
```

Testing the Implementations:

python

```python
def test_fibonacci():

    n = 10

    print(f"Fibonacci Recursive({n}): {fibonacci_recursive(n)}")

    print(f"Fibonacci Iterative({n}): {fibonacci_iterative(n)}")

    print(f"Fibonacci Memoization({n}): {fibonacci_memoization(n)}")


if __name__ == "__main__":

    test_fibonacci()
```

Sample Output:

scss

```
Fibonacci Recursive(10): 55

Fibonacci Iterative(10): 55

Fibonacci Memoization(10): 55
```

Conclusion:

By systematically breaking down the problem and applying appropriate strategies, you can effectively solve complex programming challenges.

7. Conclusion & Next Steps

Congratulations! You've completed the first chapter of *Mastering Data Structures and Algorithms with Python*. This chapter laid the groundwork by introducing the significance of Data Structures and Algorithms in software development, providing an overview of their implementation using Python, and guiding you through practical projects to solidify your understanding.

Key Takeaways:

- **Foundation of DS&A:** Grasped the essential concepts of data structures and algorithms, recognizing their critical role in efficient software development.

- **Practical Implementation:** Built hands-on projects like a dictionary application, browser history manager, and file system explorer to apply theoretical knowledge.

- **Advanced Insights:** Explored advanced topics such as heaps, tries, and algorithm optimization techniques to enhance your problem-solving toolkit.

- **Troubleshooting Skills:** Developed strategies to effectively debug and optimize your code, ensuring robustness and performance.

Next Steps:

1. **Deepen Your Knowledge:**

   o Proceed to the next chapters, which will delve into specific data structures like arrays, linked lists, stacks, queues, trees, and graphs, along with their corresponding algorithms.

2. **Engage with Practice Problems:**

   o Reinforce your learning by solving the practice problems provided at the end of each chapter. Websites like LeetCode and HackerRank offer excellent platforms for coding challenges.

3. **Build More Projects:**

   o Apply your skills to larger projects, such as developing a simple web crawler or creating a personal task manager. Practical application accelerates learning and enhances retention.

4. **Explore Optimization Techniques:**

   o Study advanced algorithm optimization strategies and learn how to analyze and improve the efficiency of your code using Big O Notation.

5. **Prepare for Technical Interviews:**

   o Utilize the knowledge gained to excel in technical interviews. Focus on common DS&A questions and practice articulating your thought process clearly and concisely.

Additional Resources:

- **Books:**

  - *"Introduction to Algorithms"* by Cormen, Leiserson, Rivest, and Stein.

  - *"Data Structures and Algorithms in Python"* by Michael T. Goodrich, Roberto Tamassia, and Michael H. Goldwasser.

- **Online Courses:**

  - Coursera's Algorithms Specialization

  - edX's Data Structures Fundamentals

- **Interactive Platforms:**

  - Visualgo.net

  - GeeksforGeeks

Final Encouragement:

Mastering Data Structures and Algorithms is a journey that requires dedication, practice, and perseverance. Embrace the challenges, celebrate your progress, and stay curious. With each concept you conquer and each project you complete, you're building a strong foundation that will empower you to create efficient, scalable, and impactful software solutions.

Remember, every expert was once a beginner. Keep pushing forward, and soon you'll find yourself navigating the complex world of software development with ease and confidence. You can do it!

CHAPTER 2: **PYTHON ESSENTIALS FOR DATA STRUCTURES AND ALGORITHMS**

T his chapter focuses on establishing a strong Python foundation specifically tailored for understanding, implementing, and optimizing Data Structures and Algorithms (DS&A). While Python is widely appreciated for its readability and rich ecosystem, certain language-specific nuances play a significant role in how efficiently you can implement core DS&A concepts. Whether you are entirely new to Python or just need a refresher, this chapter will equip you with the essentials, including basic syntax, environment setup, and the process of writing and running your first Python program. By the end, you will have a robust groundwork to explore more advanced topics in upcoming chapters, ensuring that you can leverage Python's features effectively in your DS&A journey.

1. Introduction

1.1 Why Python for Data Structures and Algorithms?

Python has gained tremendous popularity for its clear syntax and extensive standard library. From novice coders to seasoned professionals, the language is often praised for its readability and elegance—qualities that are especially valuable when learning and working with DS&A. Complex ideas become more approachable when you don't have to wrestle with convoluted syntax, letting you focus on the underlying logic instead.

- Readability   and   Simplicity
  In many languages, boilerplate code can distract from the main DS&A logic. Python's clean syntax reduces that clutter, making your algorithms more transparent and easier to debug.

- Vast   Standard   Library
  Python's standard library offers built-in data structures like lists (dynamic arrays), dictionaries (hash tables), and sets, all of which are highly optimized. This not only speeds up development but also allows you to explore DS&A concepts without having to implement everything from scratch—unless you want to for learning purposes.

- Rich   Ecosystem   of   Libraries
  Libraries such as NumPy, pandas, and matplotlib can aid in understanding performance metrics, visualizing data structures, and prototyping complex algorithmic solutions quickly. Although we'll stay relatively close to Python's built-ins in this chapter, being aware of these resources is beneficial for future exploration.

- Community   and   Documentation
  Python's large community means abundant resources—tutorials, documentation, Q&A forums—that provide immediate support if you get stuck.

1.2 What to Expect from This Chapter

This chapter aims to bridge any gaps you might have in basic Python knowledge. We'll focus on elements of the language that are most relevant to implementing data structures and algorithms. Key areas covered include:

1. Python Basics Refresher

   o Core data types (integers, floats, strings, booleans)

   o Variables, operators, and expressions

   o Control flow (conditionals, loops)

   o Functions and scope

   o Modules and packages

2. Setting Up Your Development Environment

   o Choosing the right environment (VS Code, PyCharm, Jupyter Notebook, etc.)

   o Installing Python on different platforms

- o   Using virtual environments for project isolation

- o   Essential extensions and tools for productivity

3.   Writing and Running Your First Python Program

- o   How to create a Python script

- o   Command-line execution vs. IDE-based running

- o   Troubleshooting common errors

- o   Basic project structure and best practices

By the end of this chapter, you should feel confident in your ability to write basic Python programs, understand how Python's core features map to DS&A tasks, and have a fully functional environment to begin coding. This foundation will serve as the stepping stone for more advanced projects, hands-on examples, and optimizations in subsequent chapters.

2. Core Concepts and Theory

2.1 Core Python Data Types and Structures

When implementing DS&A in Python, you'll frequently interact with a handful of core data structures. Although these are distinct from the custom data structures (like linked lists or trees) we'll build later, they form the everyday toolkit for any Python developer.

1.   Integers, Floats, and Complex Numbers

- o   Integers (int): Whole numbers (e.g., 0, 1, -5). Python 3 has long integer support by default, meaning integers can grow arbitrarily large as long as memory permits.

- o   Floats (float): Real numbers with a fractional part (e.g., 3.14, -0.001). They follow the IEEE 754 double-precision standard.

- o   Complex (complex): Numbers with a real and imaginary part (e.g., 3+4j). While not typically the focal point in DS&A, it's worth noting Python's built-in support for them.

2. **Booleans**
   Python uses True and False to represent boolean values. These often play a critical role in conditional checks within algorithms.

3. **Strings**
   Strings in Python are immutable sequences of characters. You'll often use them in algorithmic challenges that involve text processing, pattern matching, or hashing. Key points include:

   o Immutability: Once created, a string cannot be modified in-place. Operations like concatenation create new objects.

   o Slicing: Python's slice notation (str[start:end:step]) is powerful for string manipulation and sub-string extraction.

4. **Lists**
   Lists in Python are dynamic arrays that can hold elements of different data types. Their mutable nature and built-in methods (like append(), pop(), sort()) make them versatile.

   o Indexing and Slicing: Retrieve and manipulate elements using square brackets.

   o Time Complexity:

     ▪ Access by index: O(1)

     ▪ Appending: Average O(1) (amortized)

     ▪ Inserting/Removing: O(n) in the worst case (due to shifting elements).

5. **Tuples**
   Tuples are immutable sequences, often used to store collections of heterogeneous data. Because they are immutable, they can be used as dictionary keys or set elements.

6. **Dictionaries**
   Python's dictionaries are essentially hash tables, providing average O(1) time complexity for lookups, insertions, and deletions. You'll rely on dictionaries heavily for many algorithmic tasks.

7. **Sets**
   Python sets are also implemented as hash tables, storing unique elements and offering average O(1) lookup times. They're ideal for membership checks and eliminating duplicates.

2.2 Variables, Expressions, and Operators

1. Variable   Assignment
   Python uses dynamic typing, so variables don't require type declarations.
   For example:

python

```
x = 10
```

```
x = "Hello World"
```

The same variable x can hold an integer initially and later store a string without an explicit type change.

2. Arithmetic Operators

   o + (addition), - (subtraction), *** (multiplication), / (division), //
      (floor division), % (modulus), ** (exponentiation).

python

```
a = 5
```

```
b = 2
```

```
print(a + b)   # 7
```

```
print(a / b)   # 2.5
```

```
print(a // b)  # 2
```

```
print(a ** b)  # 25
```

3. Comparison and Logical Operators

   o Comparison: ==, !=, >, <, >=, <=

   o Logical: and, or, not

python

```python
print(5 > 2 and 5 < 10)   # True

print(5 == 5 or 5 == 6)   # True

print(not (5 > 2))        # False
```

4. **Identity and Membership Operators**

   o Identity: is, is not

   o Membership: in, not in

python

```python
list_a = [1, 2, 3]

list_b = list_a

print(list_a is list_b)      # True (they reference the same list)

print(2 in list_a)         # True

print(4 not in list_a)      # True
```

2.3 Control Flow

1. **Conditionals**
   The if, elif, and else statements guide the flow of your program:

python

```python
age = 20

if age < 18:

    print("Minor")

elif age < 65:

    print("Adult")
```

else:

    print("Senior")

    2.   Loops

- for Loop: Typically used for iterating over a range or iterable (like a list or string):

python

```
for i in range(3):
    print(i)  # Prints 0, 1, 2
```

- while Loop: Continues until a given condition becomes false:

python

```
i = 0
while i < 3:
    print(i)
    i += 1
```

    3.   Loop Control Statements

- break: Exits the nearest enclosing loop.

- continue: Skips the rest of the current loop iteration and moves to the next iteration.

python

```
for i in range(5):
    if i == 2:
        continue
```

```
if i == 4:

    break

print(i)  # Output: 0, 1, 3
```

2.4 Functions and Scope

1. Defining Functions

python

```
def greet(name):

    return f"Hello, {name}!"
```

- o Parameters vs. Arguments: Parameters are placeholders in function definitions, while arguments are the actual values passed.

- o Default Arguments: Provide a default value if no argument is supplied.

python

```
def greet(name="World"):

    return f"Hello, {name}!"
```

2. Variable Scope

- o Local Scope: Variables declared within a function are accessible only inside it.

- o Global Scope: Variables declared outside all functions are accessible anywhere in the file. Modifying global variables inside functions requires the global keyword, but overuse of globals is generally discouraged.

3. Lambda Functions
One-line anonymous functions are common in Python for short operations:

python

```
square = lambda x: x * x

print(square(5))  # 25
```

2.5 Modules and Packages

1. **What Are Modules and Packages?**

   o Module: A single .py file containing Python definitions and statements.

   o Package: A directory containing one or more modules, plus an __init__.py file.

2. **Importing Modules**

python

```
import math

from math import sqrt

from math import sin as sine
```

   o import math: Imports the entire math module.

   o from math import sqrt: Imports only the sqrt function.

   o import my_module: Imports a custom module named my_module.py.

3. **Creating Your Own Module**

   o Create a file named my_module.py.

   o Define some functions or variables.

   o Import it in another script using import my_module.

Modular code organization is crucial for building data structures and algorithms. It promotes reusability and maintainability, letting you separate implementations for different structures (e.g., a stack, a queue) into distinct modules.

3. Tools and Setup

3.1 Choosing the Right Environment

Developers have multiple environment choices when working with Python. Although every environment can execute Python code, different workflows and preferences might guide you to choose one IDE or code editor over another.

1. Visual Studio Code (VS Code)

   o   Pros: Lightweight, highly customizable through extensions, integrated terminal, built-in Git support, intelligent code completion (via the Python extension).

   o   Cons: Requires configuration and extensions to match the feature set of dedicated Python IDEs.

2. PyCharm

   o   Pros: Rich Python-specific features (intelligent refactoring, debugging, unit testing), strong code analysis, built-in tools for virtual environments.

   o   Cons: Heavier than code editors like VS Code and can be overwhelming for beginners.

3. Jupyter Notebook

   o   Pros: Excellent for data visualization, prototyping, and demonstration. Code cells allow interactive exploration.

   o   Cons: Not the best for larger production projects or complex file structures; limited refactoring tools.

4. Other Code Editors

- o Sublime Text, Atom, or even the basic IDLE that comes with Python can suffice for smaller tasks.

3.2 Installing Python

Most modern systems do not have Python 3 pre-installed (except some Linux distributions), so you may need to download the installer.

1. Windows Installation

   - o Visit python.org and download the latest Python 3 installer.

   - o During installation, check the box *"Add Python to PATH"*.

2. macOS Installation

   - o You can use the official installer from python.org.

   - o Alternatively, use Homebrew:

bash

brew install python

3. Linux Installation

   - o Most distributions have Python 3 in their package manager. For example, on Ubuntu/Debian:

bash

sudo apt-get update

sudo apt-get install python3 python3-pip

3.3 Setting Up a Virtual Environment

Python's versatility can lead to "dependency hell" if not managed properly. Virtual environments help isolate project-specific dependencies from your system-wide Python installation.

1.   Creating a Virtual Environment

bash

```
python3 -m venv venv
```

This creates a folder named venv containing a clean Python environment.

2.   Activating the Environment

○   Windows:

bash

```
venv\Scripts\activate
```

○   macOS/Linux:

bash

```
source venv/bin/activate
```

3.   Installing   Packages
Once activated, you can install libraries using pip without affecting other projects:

bash

```
pip install numpy pandas matplotlib
```

4.   Deactivating the Environment

bash

```
deactivate
```

3.4 Essential Extensions and Tools

1. **Python Extension (VS Code)**
   Offers IntelliSense, debugging, linting, and more.

2. **Git and GitHub Integration**
   Version control is vital for any project. Tools like GitLens for VS Code make tracking changes and commits intuitive.

3. **Linters and Formatters**

   o **Pylint, Flake8:** Check code style and potential errors.

   o **Black:** Automatically formats your code to adhere to PEP 8 style guidelines.

3.5 Project Structure Best Practices

When building large DS&A projects or libraries, organizing code is paramount. A common structure looks like this:

markdown

```
my_project/
├── data_structures/
│   ├── stack.py
│   ├── queue.py
│   └── __init__.py
├── algorithms/
│   ├── sorting.py
│   ├── search.py
│   └── __init__.py
├── tests/
│   ├── test_stack.py
```

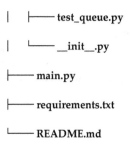

```
|     |——— test_queue.py
|     └——— __init__.py
|——— main.py
|——— requirements.txt
└——— README.md
```

- data_structures/: Contains modules for each specialized data structure.

- algorithms/: Houses algorithms like sorting, searching, graph traversals, etc.

- tests/: Stores all test files.

- main.py: Entry point for running the application or demos.

- requirements.txt: Lists project dependencies for easy installation.

- README.md: Provides an overview, usage instructions, and setup details.

This logical separation ensures maintainability and clarity, especially when working in a team or showcasing your project to recruiters.

4. Hands-on Examples & Projects

Hands-on practice cements the concepts covered in the previous sections. The following examples and mini-projects will guide you through writing and running Python code, demonstrating how to integrate Python fundamentals into DS&A-centric tasks.

4.1 Writing and Running Your First Python Program

Though simple, creating a "Hello World" script is a rite of passage that solidifies the development workflow.

4.1.1 Hello World in the Terminal

1. **Create**   a   **File**

   Create a file named hello.py in your project directory.

python

```
# hello.py

print("Hello, World!")
```

2. **Run the Script**

bash

```
python hello.py
```

Output:

```
Hello, World!
```

3. **Discussion**

   o This trivial example verifies that your Python installation and environment are working correctly.

   o If you encounter any "command not found" errors, ensure Python is properly added to your system PATH (Windows) or installed correctly (macOS/Linux).

4.1.2 Hello World in an IDE

1. **Visual Studio Code**

   o Open VS Code and install the Python extension if not already done.

   o Create or open hello.py in VS Code.

   o Run the file (typically by pressing F5 or using the "Run" button in the top-right corner).

2. **PyCharm**

- o Open PyCharm and create a new Python project.

- o Right-click hello.py and select Run 'hello'.

- o Observe the output in the console at the bottom of the PyCharm window.

3. Jupyter Notebook

- o Create a new notebook (hello.ipynb).

- o Add a code cell:

python

```python
print("Hello, World!")
```

- o Run the cell.

- o This environment displays output inline, making it interactive for experiments.

4.2 Project: A Basic Calculator

Objective:
Create a command-line calculator that performs basic arithmetic (addition, subtraction, multiplication, division, exponentiation) and demonstrates function usage, conditionals, and user input handling.

4.2.1 Project Structure

kotlin

basic_calculator/

├── calculator.py

└── __init__.py (optional, for treating the folder as a package)

4.2.2 calculator.py

```python
# calculator.py

def add(x, y):
    return x + y

def subtract(x, y):
    return x - y

def multiply(x, y):
    return x * y

def divide(x, y):
    if y == 0:
        raise ZeroDivisionError("Cannot divide by zero.")
    return x / y

def power(x, y):
    return x ** y

def menu():
    print("\n--- Basic Calculator ---")
    print("1: Addition")
```

```python
    print("2: Subtraction")

    print("3: Multiplication")

    print("4: Division")

    print("5: Exponentiation")

    print("6: Exit")


def main():

    while True:

        menu()

        choice = input("Select an operation (1-6): ").strip()


        if choice == '6':

            print("Exiting the calculator. Goodbye!")

            break


        x = float(input("Enter the first number: "))

        y = float(input("Enter the second number: "))


        if choice == '1':

            result = add(x, y)

            print(f"{x} + {y} = {result}")

        elif choice == '2':

            result = subtract(x, y)

            print(f"{x} - {y} = {result}")
```

```python
    elif choice == '3':

        result = multiply(x, y)

        print(f"{x} * {y} = {result}")

    elif choice == '4':

        try:

            result = divide(x, y)

            print(f"{x} / {y} = {result}")

        except ZeroDivisionError as e:

            print(e)

    elif choice == '5':

        result = power(x, y)

        print(f"{x}^{y} = {result}")

    else:

        print("Invalid choice. Please try again.")


if __name__ == "__main__":

    main()
```

4.2.3 Running the Calculator

1. **Command Line**

bash

```bash
cd basic_calculator
python calculator.py
```

2. **Sample Interaction**

yaml

--- Basic Calculator ---

1: Addition

2: Subtraction

3: Multiplication

4: Division

5: Exponentiation

6: Exit

Select an operation (1-6): 1

Enter the first number: 10

Enter the second number: 5

10.0 + 5.0 = 15.0

4.2.4 Concepts Highlighted

- User Input: input() function for reading user data.

- Exception Handling: Gracefully handling division by zero.

- Menu Design: A simple console menu that repeatedly prompts for operations.

4.3 Project: Simple Linear Search

Objective:
Demonstrate how a basic algorithmic approach integrates with Python fundamentals. We'll implement a linear search that scans through a list to find a target value.

4.3.1 search.py

python

```python
# search.py

def linear_search(lst, target):
    """
    Returns the index of 'target' in 'lst' if found,
    otherwise returns -1.
    """
    for index, element in enumerate(lst):
        if element == target:
            return index
    return -1


def main():
    numbers = [3, 1, 4, 1, 5, 9, 2, 6, 5]
    target = float(input("Enter a number to search for: "))
    result = linear_search(numbers, target)

    if result != -1:
        print(f"Found {target} at index {result}")
    else:
        print(f"{target} not found in the list.")


if __name__ == "__main__":
```

```
main()
```

4.3.2 Running the Linear Search

1. Save   the   file
   Place search.py in a directory of your choice.

2. Command Line

bash

```
python search.py
```

3. Sample Interaction

css

Enter a number to search for: 5

Found 5.0 at index 4

4.3.3 Concepts Highlighted

- Algorithm Implementation: Shows how to integrate basic Python syntax with a linear search approach.

- Enumerate: Simplifies loop indexing, illustrating Python's "batteries-included" philosophy.

4.4 Project: Intro to Object-Oriented Programming

Objective:
Create a simple class Car that demonstrates Python's object-oriented features, which will later be crucial for building custom data structure classes.

4.4.1 car.py

python

```python
# car.py

class Car:
    def __init__(self, make, model, year):
        self.make = make
        self.model = model
        self.year = year
        self.is_running = False

    def start(self):
        if not self.is_running:
            self.is_running = True
            print(f"The {self.year} {self.make} {self.model} is now running.")
        else:
            print(f"The {self.year} {self.make} {self.model} is already running.")

    def stop(self):
        if self.is_running:
            self.is_running = False
            print(f"The {self.year} {self.make} {self.model} has stopped.")
        else:
            print(f"The {self.year} {self.make} {self.model} is already off.")
```

```python
    def drive(self):

        if self.is_running:

            print(f"The {self.year} {self.make} {self.model} is driving.")

        else:

            print(f"Start the {self.year} {self.make} {self.model} before driving.")


def main():

    # Create car instances

    car1 = Car("Toyota", "Camry", 2020)

    car2 = Car("Tesla", "Model S", 2022)


    # Interact with car1

    car1.drive()  # Should instruct to start the car first

    car1.start()

    car1.drive()

    car1.stop()


    # Interact with car2

    car2.start()

    car2.drive()

    car2.stop()


if __name__ == "__main__":

    main()
```

4.4.2 Concepts Highlighted

- **Classes and Objects:** Classes encapsulate data (attributes) and behaviors (methods).

- **__init__ Method:** Python's constructor for initializing objects.

- **Access Modifiers:** Python doesn't enforce private or protected attributes at the language level, but the naming convention _attribute signals non-public usage.

4.5 Integrating Everything: A Mini DS&A Playground

As a culminating exercise, let's create a "playground" script that demonstrates some basic DS&A operations in Python, utilizing the knowledge from the preceding sections.

4.5.1 ds_playground.py

python

ds_playground.py

```python
def display_menu():
    print("\n--- DS&A Playground ---")
    print("1. List Operations")
    print("2. Dictionary Operations")
    print("3. Set Operations")
    print("4. Linear Search in a List")
    print("5. Basic Calculator")
    print("6. Exit")
```

```python
def list_operations():
    nums = [10, 20, 30, 40, 50]
    print(f"Initial list: {nums}")
    nums.append(60)
    print(f"After append(60): {nums}")
    nums.remove(20)
    print(f"After remove(20): {nums}")
    nums.insert(1, 15)
    print(f"After insert(1, 15): {nums}")
    print(f"Sorted list: {sorted(nums)}")


def dictionary_operations():
    phone_book = {
        "Alice": "123-456-7890",
        "Bob": "987-654-3210",
        "Charlie": "555-555-5555"
    }
    print(f"Initial dictionary: {phone_book}")
    phone_book["Diana"] = "222-333-4444"
    print(f"After adding Diana: {phone_book}")
    del phone_book["Bob"]
    print(f"After deleting Bob: {phone_book}")
    print(f"Alice's number: {phone_book.get('Alice')}")
```

```python
def set_operations():
    fruits = {"apple", "banana", "cherry"}
    print(f"Initial set: {fruits}")
    fruits.add("date")
    print(f"After add('date'): {fruits}")
    fruits.discard("banana")
    print(f"After discard('banana'): {fruits}")
    print(f"Is 'apple' in fruits? {'apple' in fruits}")


def linear_search_demo():
    numbers = [5, 3, 8, 2, 7, 1, 9]
    target = int(input("Enter a number to search for in [5,3,8,2,7,1,9]: "))
    for index, element in enumerate(numbers):
        if element == target:
            print(f"Found {target} at index {index}")
            return
    print(f"{target} not found in the list.")


def basic_calculator_demo():
    x = float(input("Enter the first number: "))
    y = float(input("Enter the second number: "))
    operation = input("Choose an operation (+, -, *, /, ^): ")
```

```python
    if operation == '+':

        print(f"{x} + {y} = {x + y}")

    elif operation == '-':

        print(f"{x} - {y} = {x - y}")

    elif operation == '*':

        print(f"{x} * {y} = {x * y}")

    elif operation == '/':

        if y == 0:

            print("Error: Cannot divide by zero.")

        else:

            print(f"{x} / {y} = {x / y}")

    elif operation == '^':

        print(f"{x}^{y} = {x ** y}")

    else:

        print("Invalid operation.")


def main():

    while True:

        display_menu()

        choice = input("Enter your choice (1-6): ")


        if choice == '1':

            list_operations()

        elif choice == '2':
```

```python
        dictionary_operations()

    elif choice == '3':

        set_operations()

    elif choice == '4':

        linear_search_demo()

    elif choice == '5':

        basic_calculator_demo()

    elif choice == '6':

        print("Exiting DS&A Playground.")

        break

    else:

        print("Invalid choice. Please try again.")


if __name__ == "__main__":

    main()
```

4.5.2 Running the DS&A Playground

1. **Execution:**

bash

```bash
python ds_playground.py
```

2. **Exploration:**

   o Perform list operations (append, remove, insert, sort).

   o Manipulate a dictionary (add, delete, retrieve).

   o Use a set (add, remove elements, membership test).

o   Try out a simple linear search.

o   Test the basic calculator functionality.

4.5.3 Concepts Reinforced

- Integration: Demonstrates how core Python features—lists, dictionaries, sets, input handling—coalesce in a single program.

- Practical DS&A: Provides a springboard to more advanced projects, showing how to structure code and keep it modular.

5. Advanced Techniques & Optimization

Though the projects so far have been introductory, Python's flexibility and performance can be extended further through certain best practices and advanced techniques. Let's explore some key insights for efficient Python coding in DS&A contexts.

5.1 List Comprehensions and Generator Expressions

1.   List Comprehensions

A concise way to construct lists. Useful for quickly creating test data or transforming existing lists.

python

```
squares = [x*x for x in range(10)]
```

Equivalent to:

python

```python
squares = []

for x in range(10):

  squares.append(x*x)
```

2. **Generator**   **Expressions**
   Similar to list comprehensions, but produce values on-the-fly, which is memory-efficient for large datasets.

python

```python
squares_gen = (x*x for x in range(10))

print(next(squares_gen))  # 0

print(next(squares_gen))  # 1
```

5.2 Lambda Functions in Higher-Order Operations

1. Map, Filter, and Reduce

   o Map: Applies a function to every item of an iterable:

python

```python
numbers = [1, 2, 3, 4, 5]

doubled = list(map(lambda x: x * 2, numbers))
```

   o Filter: Filters items out of an iterable based on a condition:

python

```python
even = list(filter(lambda x: x % 2 == 0, numbers))
```

      o   Reduce: Accumulates a result by applying a function cumulatively:

python

from functools import reduce

sum_of_numbers = reduce(lambda acc, x: acc + x, numbers, 0)

   2.   Use Cases in DS&A

      o   Map: Data transformations before applying an algorithm (e.g., convert all strings to lowercase).

      o   Filter: Preprocessing steps to include only the elements that matter.

      o   Reduce: Aggregating partial results, like summing an array or computing a product.

5.3 Built-in Functions and Libraries for Performance

   1.   bisect   Module
      Implements an algorithm for maintaining a sorted list in Python. Particularly helpful for binary insertion:

python

import bisect

my_list = [1, 2, 4, 5]

bisect.insort(my_list, 3)

print(my_list) # [1, 2, 3, 4, 5]

   2.   collections Module

- o   deque: A highly optimized list-like container with fast appends and pops on both ends (O(1)).

- o   Counter: Tallies elements in an iterable, useful for frequency-based problems.

- o   defaultdict: Simplifies dictionary usage when default values are needed.

3.   array   Module
For numeric arrays with fixed types, more memory-efficient than Python lists. Useful when you have large collections of numbers and need performance.

5.4 Profiling and Benchmarking

1.   time   Module
Simple to use for rough performance measurements:

python

```
import time

start = time.time()
# Code to measure
end = time.time()
print(f"Execution time: {end - start} seconds")
```

2.   timeit   Module
Provides more precise benchmarking by running the code snippet multiple times:

python

```
import timeit
```

```
setup_code = "from __main__ import linear_search, numbers"

test_code = "linear_search(numbers, 5)"

execution_time = timeit.timeit(stmt=test_code, setup=setup_code, number=1000)

print(f"Execution time over 1000 runs: {execution_time} seconds")
```

3. Profilers

    o   cProfile: Built-in profiler for Python that gives detailed stats about function calls and execution time.

    o   Line Profiler: A third-party tool that profiles line-by-line.

5.5 Memory Management and Optimization

1. Reference   Counting
    Python uses reference counting to manage memory. When an object's reference count drops to zero, it's eligible for garbage collection.

2. Object   Interning
    Small integers and strings are often *interned*, meaning they can be reused to optimize memory usage.

3. Efficient Data Structures

    o   Avoid Unnecessary Copies: For large lists, slicing creates a new list in memory. Use itertools.islice or generator expressions to handle slicing on-the-fly.

    o   Mutable vs. Immutable: Sometimes, using immutable data (like tuples) can avoid overhead when passing data around, but mutability can be beneficial in other scenarios.

6. Troubleshooting and Problem-Solving

Even simple Python scripts can pose challenges, especially when you're just getting started. This section highlights common pitfalls and strategies to solve them.

6.1 Common Errors in Python

1. Syntax Errors

    o   Example: Missing a colon after an if statement or forgetting parentheses.

    o   Solution: Read the traceback carefully and correct the syntax near the indicated line.

2. Name Errors

    o   Example: Misspelling a variable or function name.

    o   Solution: Make sure the variable is defined in the correct scope. Double-check your spelling.

3. Type Errors

    o   Example: Attempting to concatenate a string with an integer ("Hello" + 5).

    o   Solution: Convert types when necessary (str(5)) or confirm the data type of variables before operations.

4. Index Errors

    o   Example: Accessing an index that doesn't exist in a list.

    o   Solution: Use len(list) checks or handle out-of-range scenarios gracefully.

5. Key Errors (Dictionaries)

    o   Example: Trying to access a non-existent dictionary key.

    o   Solution: Use dict.get(key, default) to handle missing keys or check membership with if key in dict.

6.2 Debugging Techniques

1. Print Statements

   A simple yet powerful way to see what's happening under the hood. Print the values of variables at various points to isolate the issue.

2. IDE Debuggers

   Step through code line by line, inspect variables, and watch the call stack in real-time. Tools like PyCharm, VS Code, and Jupyter have built-in debuggers.

3. Unit Tests

   Writing tests ensures that functions behave as expected. If a test fails, you have a direct pointer to what's broken.

4. Rubber Duck Debugging

   Explaining the problem to a "rubber duck" (or any inanimate object or colleague) can often clarify your logic and reveal errors.

6.3 Handling Exceptions Gracefully

1. try-except Blocks

python

```
try:
  result = divide(10, 0)
except ZeroDivisionError as e:
  print(e)
```

2. Multiple Exceptions

python

```
try:
```

```python
result = some_function()
```

```python
except (ValueError, TypeError) as e:

    print("Value or Type Error occurred.", e)
```

3. Using   finally
   Executes code regardless of whether an exception was raised, useful for cleanup:

python

```python
try:

    file = open("data.txt")

    # some operations

except FileNotFoundError:

    print("File not found!")

finally:

    file.close()
```

6.4 Problem-Solving Strategies

1. **Break Down Tasks**

   When implementing a data structure or algorithm, work incrementally. Write small functions, test them, then move on.

2. **Seek Feedback Loops**

   Continuous integration, code reviews, or pair programming can catch errors early.

3. **Leverage Online Resources**

   Communities like Stack Overflow or official Python documentation can be invaluable when you're stuck.

4. Keep Code Modular

    A well-structured codebase isolates issues more effectively. Debugging smaller modules is simpler than debugging one massive script.

7. Conclusion & Next Steps

7.1 Recap of Key Lessons

1. Python Basics

    You revisited Python's core syntax, data types, and control flow constructs — indispensable for any DS&A implementation.

2. Environment Setup

    A stable, organized development environment lays the foundation for successful coding. Properly configured tools save time and reduce errors.

3. First Python Program

    Writing a "Hello World" may be simple, but it ensures that your setup works and you're ready to dive deeper into complex tasks.

4. Hands-on Projects

    Practical mini-projects, from a basic calculator to a DS&A playground, showcased how Python fundamentals tie into algorithmic thinking.

7.2 Practical Takeaways

- Efficiency Through Pythonic Code: Leveraging list comprehensions, generators, and built-in modules can produce concise and performant solutions.

- Testing and Debugging: Regular testing, whether through simple print statements or robust unit tests, is key to reliable code.

- Object-Oriented Approach: Classes provide a neat way to encapsulate data and behaviors, making it easier to scale to more complex data structures.

7.3 Next Steps

With a solid foundation in Python and a working environment, you are now ready to tackle the core data structures—arrays, linked lists, stacks, queues, trees, graphs—and the algorithms that operate on them. Here's what lies ahead:

1. Deep Dive into Data Structures:

   Subsequent chapters will guide you through implementing fundamental data structures from scratch, enhancing your comprehension of their internal workings.

2. Algorithm Analysis:

   You'll learn to measure the efficiency of your code using Big O notation and apply best practices to optimize performance.

3. Real-World Applications:

   Examples will shift from purely theoretical exercises to more realistic scenarios, such as pathfinding, scheduling, and data retrieval.

4. Interview Preparation:

   Mastery of DS&A is essential for technical interviews. As you progress, keep refining your understanding and practice solving time-bound challenges.

7.4 Additional Resources

- Official Python Documentation:

  docs.python.org for in-depth exploration of modules, data structures, and language features.

- Online Tutorials:

  Platforms like Real Python and GeeksforGeeks offer tutorials and code snippets that supplement your learning.

- Practice Platforms:

    o LeetCode: Focus on DS&A challenges.

    o HackerRank: Offers multiple difficulty levels and language-specific solutions.

7.5 Final Encouragement

Your journey with Python and DS&A has just begun. Embrace the iterative learning process—building small projects, debugging, optimizing—and soon you'll be constructing complex data structures and algorithms with confidence. Remember, every expert once started with "Hello World." Stay curious, keep experimenting, and allow your passion for problem-solving to guide you forward.

Pro Tip: Maintain a project portfolio on GitHub or similar platforms. Not only does this help you track your progress, but it also showcases your abilities to potential employers or collaborators.

With this solid groundwork, you're now well-equipped to move on to more advanced data structures and the fascinating world of algorithmic challenges. Onward to the next chapter in your DS&A mastery!

CHAPTER 3:
FUNDAMENTAL DATA STRUCTURES – ARRAYS, LISTS, AND HASH TABLES

I n this chapter, we explore three foundational data structures—**Arrays**, **Lists**, and **Hash Tables**—which form the bedrock of efficient data handling in many software systems. While arrays and lists provide ways to store and organize sequential data, hash tables make it possible to retrieve, insert, and remove elements in near-constant time by mapping keys to array positions via hashing. By the chapter's end, you will have a deep understanding of:

1. **Understanding Arrays and Lists**

   o   What arrays are and how they differ from lists

   o   How Python's built-in list type functions as a dynamic array

2. **The Concept of Hashing**

   o   How hashing works to enable near O(1) lookups

   o   Common collision resolution strategies

3. **Common Operations and Use Cases**

   o   Real-world applications of arrays, lists, and hash tables

   o   Which data structure to choose for a given scenario

4. **Implementing Dynamic Arrays and Hash Tables in Python**

   o   A closer look at Python's list as a dynamic array

o   Building a rudimentary hash table from scratch

5. **Project: Creating a Simple Dictionary Application**

o   Step-by-step guide to designing a console-based dictionary app

o   Demonstration of how hash tables underpin Python dictionaries

By mastering these concepts, you will gain the confidence and expertise to store and retrieve data efficiently, laying a strong foundation for more advanced data structures and algorithms in future chapters.

1. Introduction

Data structures serve as the skeleton of any software application—without them, dealing with large volumes of data would be chaotic, resource-intensive, and slow. Among the core structures, arrays and lists provide the backbone for linear data, while hash tables open the door to near-instant lookups. Whether you are coding a web service that needs to manage user sessions, a machine learning pipeline analyzing massive datasets, or a game engine that tracks player entities, these three data structures will appear under the hood in one form or another.

Why Focus on Arrays, Lists, and Hash Tables?

- **Fundamental Building Blocks:** Arrays are some of the simplest data structures, often taught in introductory programming courses because they closely map to memory usage at a low level. Lists in Python build on top of arrays, introducing flexibility by dynamically resizing and offering built-in methods for manipulation.

- **Universal Relevance:** Hash tables (and by extension, Python dictionaries) are widely used in countless applications, from caching to indexing, because they provide average-case constant time complexity for CRUD operations (Create, Read, Update, Delete).

- **Transition to Advanced Structures:** Mastery of arrays and hash tables paves the way for advanced structures like balanced trees, tries, priority queues, and graph adjacency lists. A firm command of these fundamentals is essential before tackling more complex topics.

Chapter Roadmap

First, we will dissect arrays: their strengths, weaknesses, and how they are used in low-level memory. We then transition to Python's list, explaining how it functions internally and offering a deeper dive into dynamic resizing. From there, we explore the concept of hashing—arguably one of the most clever methods in CS for enabling near O(1) lookups. We will then compare scenarios where arrays/lists excel versus where hash tables dominate. Finally, we bring everything together in a project that demonstrates the power of hash-based lookups by building a simple dictionary application.

Embrace the practical examples and code snippets as checkpoints that reinforce your understanding. By applying these data structures to real-world tasks, you transform the material from abstract theory into tangible skills you can use immediately in your coding projects.

2. Understanding Arrays and Lists

2.1 What Is an Array?

An **array** is a contiguous block of memory that holds multiple elements of the same type. Each element in the array is placed adjacent to the next, allowing for constant-time ($O(1)O(1)O(1)$) access by index. Arrays are one of the most primitive data structures, directly mapping to how data might be laid out in memory at the hardware level.

Key Characteristics of Arrays

1. **Fixed Size:** When you create an array, you typically must specify its size upfront. This size remains constant throughout the array's lifetime.

2. **Random Access:** Accessing the element at index iii is constant time. If you know the base address of the array in memory (e.g., base_address), an element at index iii can be found at base_address + (i * element_size).

3. **Efficient Iteration:** Because elements are stored contiguously, iterating through an array is cache-friendly, which can be extremely fast at scale.

Array	Example	(Conceptual)

Suppose we have an array of 5 integers:

Index 0 1 2 3 4

Value 10 20 30 40 50

- **Access**: Retrieving array[2] gives you 30 instantly, in $O(1)O(1)O(1)$ time.

- **Insertion/Deletion**: If you need to insert a new element at index 2, existing elements after that index must shift right. This is costly, taking $O(n)O(n)O(n)$ time in the worst case.

In many low-level languages like C, you deal with arrays directly, specifying their size and type. In Python, we rely on higher-level structures like list, though arrays do exist in modules such as array and numpy.

2.2 Arrays in Python

Python's standard library has a module named array that provides an array interface similar to that in C. However, its usage is less common in everyday Python coding because the built-in list type is more flexible. Here's a quick illustration of using Python's array module:

python

import array

Create an array of integers (typecode 'i' means signed integer)

numbers = array.array('i', [10, 20, 30, 40, 50])

Access and print

print(numbers[2]) # 30

Attempt insertion

numbers.insert(2, 25)

```
print(numbers)  # array('i', [10, 20, 25, 30, 40, 50])
```

Though array.array is memory-efficient and ensures all elements share a type, it doesn't resize automatically in the same sense as lists.

2.3 What Are Lists in Python?

In Python, a **list** is a built-in data structure that functions similarly to a dynamic array. It can grow and shrink on-demand, and it can store objects of different types side by side (though typically used in a uniform manner for clarity and performance considerations).

Key Characteristics of Python Lists

1. **Dynamic Resizing:** When you append an element to a list that has no extra capacity, Python allocates a larger chunk of memory, copies over the existing elements, and then adds the new element.

2. **Mixed Data Types:** You can store an integer, string, float, or even a custom object in the same list, though mixing types can have performance implications.

3. **Common Operations:**

    o **Appending:** list.append(item)

    o **Inserting:** list.insert(index, item)

    o **Removing:** list.remove(item) or del list[index]

    o **Slicing:** sub_list = list[start:end:step]

Although Python's lists are more flexible than static arrays, they maintain the contiguous memory approach under the hood, leading to $O(1)O(1)O(1)$ average-time indexing and $O(n)O(n)O(n)$ worst-case insertions or deletions in the middle of the list.

List Example

python

```
numbers = [10, 20, 30, 40, 50]

print(numbers[2])  # 30
```

```
numbers.append(60)  # Increases the list size by 1

numbers.insert(2, 25)  # Shifts elements from index 2 to the right

print(numbers)  # [10, 20, 25, 30, 40, 50, 60]


del numbers[3]

print(numbers)  # [10, 20, 25, 40, 50, 60]
```

2.4 Advantages and Disadvantages

Arrays

- **Advantages**:

    o   Predictable, contiguous memory usage.

    o   Efficient random access in $O(1)O(1)O(1)$.

    o   Great for performance-sensitive tasks (especially in lower-level languages).

- **Disadvantages**:

    o   Fixed size can lead to wasted space or out-of-bound errors if not carefully managed.

    o   Inserting or removing elements (except at the end) can be $O(n)O(n)O(n)$.

Lists

- **Advantages**:

    o   Flexible sizing.

    o   Built-in methods for common operations.

    o   Still provides $O(1)O(1)O(1)$ average-time indexing.

- **Disadvantages**:

  o   Potential overhead from dynamic resizing.

  o   Type flexibility can lead to subtle errors if not used carefully.

  o   Still has $O(n)O(n)O(n)$ complexity for mid-list insertions and deletions in the worst case.

When to Use Them

- **Arrays**: Ideal when you need a fixed-size container with guaranteed $O(1)O(1)O(1)$ indexing and minimal overhead. Often used in performance-critical or memory-constrained contexts.

- **Python Lists**: A go-to choice for everyday coding in Python, as they handle the majority of array-like use cases gracefully with minimal manual management.

3. The Concept of Hashing

3.1 Why Hashing Matters

Imagine you want to store a collection of "key-value" pairs, such as usernames mapped to email addresses. You could place each pair in a list and search linearly for a matching key. However, linear search for each lookup yields $O(n)O(n)O(n)$ complexity, which grows unwieldy as n becomes large.

Hashing offers a more optimal way to find items based on a key—typically in $O(1)O(1)O(1)$ average time. This is accomplished by using a **hash function** to convert a key into an integer (its "hash"), which is then mapped to an index in an underlying array.

3.2 Hash Function Basics

A **hash function** is any function hhh that maps data (often strings or numbers) to a pseudo-random integer. For a key kkk, the index in the hash table is calculated as:

index=h(k)mod table_size\text{index}   =   h(k)   \mod \text{table_size}index=h(k)modtable_size

Desirable Properties of a Hash Function

1. **Deterministic**: Same key always produces the same hash.

2. **Uniform Distribution**: Hashes should be well-distributed to minimize collisions.

3. **Efficiency**: Computing the hash function should be fast.

3.3 Handling Collisions

Collision: Occurs when two different keys hash to the same index. Collisions are inevitable due to the pigeonhole principle—if there are more keys than slots, at least two keys must land in the same slot. Common strategies for dealing with collisions include:

1. **Chaining (Open Hashing)**

   Each slot in the table points to a list (or another structure) of items that share the same index. If collisions are not excessive, lookup within the chain remains close to constant time on average.

2. **Open Addressing (Closed Hashing)**

   Instead of using a linked list, each collision prompts the algorithm to probe other positions in the array until an empty slot is found. Methods like **linear probing, quadratic probing**, and **double hashing** belong here.

3. **Perfect Hashing**

   In specialized scenarios where the data set is known in advance and minimal collisions are desired, perfect hashing techniques can ensure collisions never occur.

3.4 Hash Tables in Practice

A **hash table** (also called a **hash map**) typically uses an underlying array, with each entry corresponding to a "bucket." When we insert a key-value pair, the key is hashed to determine the bucket index. If a collision occurs, the item might be appended to a chain or placed in the next available location, depending on the strategy used.

Real-World Example: Library System

A library must map ISBN numbers (keys) to information about each book (values). A hash-based approach allows librarians (or the system) to look up a book's details quickly. Each ISBN is hashed, and the index points to the location where the book record is stored.

3.5 Hashing in Python

In Python, dictionaries (dict) and sets (set) rely on hash tables under the hood. When you do something like:

python

phone_book = {}

phone_book["Alice"] = "123-456-7890"

Python computes a hash for the string "Alice", then uses that to place the value "123-456-7890" in an internal array-based structure, handling collisions automatically.

4. Common Operations and Use Cases

4.1 Arrays/Lists: Operations and Applications

1. **Access by Index**

   o **Time Complexity**: $O(1)O(1)O(1)$ for both arrays and Python lists.

   o **Example**: Retrieving the 3rd element in a list of 1,000,000 items is just as fast as retrieving it in a list of 10.

2. **Insertion at the End**

   o **Arrays**: Often not possible if the array is at capacity.

- Python Lists: Average $O(1)O(1)O(1)$ (amortized) if there is spare capacity; occasionally triggers resizing, which can be $O(n)O(n)O(n)$ but infrequent.

3. **Insertion/Deletion in the Middle**

- **Both**: Potentially $O(n)O(n)O(n)$ because elements need to shift.

4. **Use Cases**

- **Arrays**: Great in memory-critical scenarios or when you know the exact size in advance.

- **Lists**: Default choice in Python for iterative or dynamic data handling.

Real-World Examples

- **Working with Sensor Data**: If a device logs sensor readings in real time, appending to a Python list is straightforward and efficient for later batch processing.

- **Batch Data Processing**: Arrays in lower-level languages handle large, fixed datasets quickly (e.g., image processing, where the dimensions are set).

4.2 Hash Tables: Operations and Applications

1. **Insertion**

- Compute key's hash index and place the item. If a collision occurs, handle according to your collision strategy.

- Average $O(1)O(1)O(1)$, worst-case $O(n)O(n)O(n)$ if collisions cluster or degrade to chaining.

2. **Lookup**

- Compute key's hash, jump directly to that index, then traverse a short chain or do a quick open addressing check.

- Average $O(1)O(1)O(1)$, worst-case $O(n)O(n)O(n)$.

3. **Deletion**

    o   Similar to insertion: Find the item via its hash, remove it from that
        location.

    o   Average $O(1)O(1)O(1)$, worst-case $O(n)O(n)O(n)$.

4. **Use Cases**

    o   **Caching**: Storing frequently accessed data for quick retrieval.

    o   **Database Indexing**: Maintaining quick lookups for search keys.

    o   **Symbol Tables in Compilers**: Mapping variable names to memory
        locations.

Real-World Examples

*   **DNS Resolvers**: Map domain names (keys) to IP addresses (values).

*   **Language Dictionaries**: Translate words from one language to another swiftly.

5. Implementing Dynamic Arrays and Hash Tables in Python

While Python's built-in list and dict already handle dynamic resizing and hashing,
implementing simplified versions yourself deepens your understanding of how they
work under the hood. This section guides you through a minimal dynamic array and a
basic hash table from scratch.

5.1 Building a Simple Dynamic Array in Python

Disclaimer: Python lists are effectively dynamic arrays already. We'll do a conceptual
example to illustrate the underlying mechanics.

5.1.1 Class Structure

python

```python
class DynamicArray:

    def __init__(self):

        self.capacity = 1

        self.count = 0

        self.array = self.make_array(self.capacity)


    def __len__(self):

        return self.count


    def __getitem__(self, index):

        if not 0 <= index < self.count:

            raise IndexError("Index out of range")

        return self.array[index]


    def append(self, value):

        if self.count == self.capacity:

            self._resize(2 * self.capacity)

        self.array[self.count] = value

        self.count += 1

    def _resize(self, new_capacity):

        new_array = self.make_array(new_capacity)

        for i in range(self.count):

            new_array[i] = self.array[i]
```

```python
        self.array = new_array

        self.capacity = new_capacity


    def make_array(self, size):

        # A low-level approach: return an array of references

        return [None] * size
```

1. **Initialization**: Start with a capacity of 1 and a count of 0.

2. **Access/Index**: The __getitem__ magic method allows us to use square bracket notation.

3. **Appending**: If the array is full, resize to double the current capacity (amortized O(1)O(1)O(1) time complexity).

4. **Resizing**: Allocate a new array with double the size, elements over, and point self.array to the new space.

5.1.2 Testing the Dynamic Array

python

```python
def test_dynamic_array():

    arr = DynamicArray()

    arr.append(10)

    arr.append(20)

    arr.append(30)

    arr.append(40)


    print("Length:", len(arr))  # 4

    for i in range(len(arr)):

        print(arr[i])
```

```
# 10, 20, 30, 40


if __name__ == "__main__":

    test_dynamic_array()
```

In practice, you will almost always use Python's built-in list, but seeing how a simplified version works is instructive.

5.2 Building a Simple Hash Table in Python

Let's create a rudimentary hash table using **chaining** for collisions.

5.2.1 Hash Table Structure

python

```
class HashTable:

    def __init__(self, capacity=10):

        self.capacity = capacity

        self.size = 0

        # Each bucket holds a list of (key, value) pairs

        self.buckets = [[] for _ in range(capacity)]


    def hash_func(self, key):

        """Compute a simple hash value for the given key."""

        return hash(key) % self.capacity


    def insert(self, key, value):
```

```python
        index = self.hash_func(key)

        # Check if key already exists; if so, update it

        for i, (k, v) in enumerate(self.buckets[index]):

            if k == key:

                self.buckets[index][i] = (key, value)

                return

        # Otherwise, insert a new (key, value) pair

        self.buckets[index].append((key, value))

        self.size += 1


        # Optional: resize if load factor is too high

        if self.size / self.capacity > 0.7:

            self._resize()


    def get(self, key):

        index = self.hash_func(key)

        for (k, v) in self.buckets[index]:

            if k == key:

                return v

        return None  # Key not found


    def remove(self, key):

        index = self.hash_func(key)

        for i, (k, v) in enumerate(self.buckets[index]):
```

```python
            if k == key:

                del self.buckets[index][i]

                self.size -= 1

                return True

        return False  # Key not found


    def _resize(self):
        """Resize the hash table to double its current capacity."""
        new_capacity = self.capacity * 2

        new_buckets = [[] for _ in range(new_capacity)]


        # Rehash existing items

        for bucket in self.buckets:

            for (k, v) in bucket:

                new_index = hash(k) % new_capacity

                new_buckets[new_index].append((k, v))


        self.capacity = new_capacity

        self.buckets = new_buckets
```

1. **Initialization**: We start with a certain capacity (default 10) and create a list of empty lists (buckets).

2. **hash_func**: Uses Python's built-in hash() function, reduced modulo our capacity.

3. **insert**:

    o   Find the correct bucket.

- o Update value if key already exists; otherwise append a new pair.

- o Increase size and resize if load factor (size/capacity) exceeds 0.7.

4. **get**: Find the correct bucket, linearly scan for the key, and return the associated value if found.

5. **remove**: Scan the bucket for the key, remove it, and decrease size.

6. **_resize**: Double the capacity and rehash all existing elements.

5.2.2 Testing the Hash Table

python

```python
def test_hash_table():

    ht = HashTable()


    # Insert data

    ht.insert("apple", 1)

    ht.insert("banana", 2)

    ht.insert("orange", 3)


    print(ht.get("apple"))  # 1

    print(ht.get("banana"))  # 2

    print(ht.get("grape"))  # None (not found)


    # Update value

    ht.insert("apple", 100)

    print(ht.get("apple"))  # 100
```

```python
# Remove data

success = ht.remove("banana")

print(success)        # True

print(ht.get("banana"))  # None (removed)


if __name__ == "__main__":

    test_hash_table()
```

Output:

mathematica

1

2

None

100

True

None

This simplistic hash table demonstrates the core principles of hashing, collision handling (chaining), and resizing. Python dictionaries, of course, are highly optimized versions of this concept.

6. Project: Creating a Simple Dictionary Application

In this final section, we apply our knowledge of lists (for user interaction) and hash tables (for storing key-value data) to build a simple console-based dictionary application. Although you could accomplish this easily with Python's built-in dict, we'll demonstrate how you might structure such an app and optionally plug in our custom HashTable class if you wish.

6.1 Project Overview

Our application will store word definitions. The user can:

- **Add a new word**

- **Search for a definition**

- **Delete a word**

- **List all words**

- **Exit**

We'll rely on the built-in Python dict for simplicity, but you can swap in your custom HashTable if you want to practice.

High-Level Design

sql


```
+---------------------------+

| Dictionary Application  |

| (console-based)       |

|                |

| Operations:        |

| - Add word         |

| - Search word       |

| - Delete word       |

| - List all words      |

| - Exit           |
```

```
+-------------------------+
            |
            v
+-------------------------+
| Python dict or HashTable |
| {word -> definition}     |
+-------------------------+
```

6.2 Step-by-Step Implementation

Create a Python file named dictionary_app.py.

python

```python
# dictionary_app.py


def display_menu():
    print("\n----- My Dictionary App -----")
    print("1. Add a new word")
    print("2. Search for a word")
    print("3. Delete a word")
    print("4. List all words")
    print("5. Exit")


def add_word(my_dict):
    word = input("Enter the word: ").strip()
```

```python
    if word in my_dict:
        print(f"'{word}' already exists.")
        return

    definition = input("Enter the definition: ").strip()
    my_dict[word] = definition
    print(f"Word '{word}' added successfully.")


def search_word(my_dict):
    word = input("Enter the word to search: ").strip()
    if word in my_dict:
        print(f"{word} : {my_dict[word]}")
    else:
        print(f"'{word}' not found.")


def delete_word(my_dict):
    word = input("Enter the word to delete: ").strip()
    if word in my_dict:
        del my_dict[word]
        print(f"'{word}' deleted successfully.")
    else:
        print(f"'{word}' not found.")


def list_all_words(my_dict):
```

```python
    if not my_dict:

        print("Dictionary is empty.")

        return


    print("\nCurrent words in the dictionary:")

    for word, definition in my_dict.items():

        print(f"{word} : {definition}")


def main():

    # You can replace 'my_dict = {}' with 'my_dict = HashTable()'

    # if you want to use the custom hash table.

    my_dict = {}


    while True:

        display_menu()

        choice = input("Choose an option (1-5): ").strip()


        if choice == '1':

            add_word(my_dict)

        elif choice == '2':

            search_word(my_dict)

        elif choice == '3':

            delete_word(my_dict)

        elif choice == '4':
```

```python
        list_all_words(my_dict)

    elif choice == '5':

        print("Exiting the Dictionary Application...")

        break

    else:

        print("Invalid choice. Please try again.")


if __name__ == "__main__":

    main()
```

6.3 Testing the Application

1. **Run the Script**

bash

```
python dictionary_app.py
```

2. **Sample Interaction**

sql

```
----- My Dictionary App -----

1. Add a new word

2. Search for a word

3. Delete a word

4. List all words
```

5. Exit

Choose an option (1-5): 1

Enter the word: Python

Enter the definition: A high-level, interpreted programming language

Word 'Python' added successfully.

----- My Dictionary App -----

1. Add a new word

2. Search for a word

3. Delete a word

4. List all words

5. Exit

Choose an option (1-5): 2

Enter the word to search: Python

Python : A high-level, interpreted programming language

----- My Dictionary App -----

1. Add a new word

2. Search for a word

3. Delete a word

4. List all words

5. Exit

Choose an option (1-5): 4

Current words in the dictionary:

Python : A high-level, interpreted programming language

6.4 Adding Optional Features

1. **Saving to a File**

    o   Implement a feature to save the dictionary to a JSON file so the data persists across sessions.

python

```python
import json


def save_to_file(my_dict, filename="dictionary_data.json"):

    with open(filename, "w") as f:

        json.dump(my_dict, f)

    print(f"Dictionary saved to {filename}")
```

2. **Loading from a File**

python

```python
def load_from_file(filename="dictionary_data.json"):

    import os

    if os.path.exists(filename):

        with open(filename, "r") as f:

            return json.load(f)

    return {}
```

3. **Auto-Save**   **on**   **Exit**
    In the main() function, before exiting:

python

```python
save_to_file(my_dict)
```

4. **Updating**   **Definitions**
    Currently, if a word already exists, we do not update its definition. You can
    modify add_word(my_dict) to prompt the user whether to overwrite.

6.5 Using the Custom HashTable

To deepen your understanding of how hash tables work in a real application, you can
replace my_dict = {} with your custom HashTable:

python

```python
# dictionary_app.py


from hashtable import HashTable   # Assuming you named the previous code hashtable.py


def main():
    my_dict = HashTable()  # Instead of a regular dict


    while True:
        display_menu()

        choice = input("Choose an option (1-5): ").strip()
```

```
if choice == '1':

    word = input("Enter the word: ").strip()

    if my_dict.get(word) is not None:

        print(f"'{word}' already exists.")

        continue

    definition = input("Enter the definition: ").strip()

    my_dict.insert(word, definition)

    print(f"Word '{word}' added successfully.")

# ... and so forth for search, delete, list operations ...
```

This switch allows you to see your own hash table in action. You'll observe the same interface from the user's perspective, but behind the scenes, collisions and resizing get handled by your HashTable class.

7. Conclusion & Next Steps

7.1 Key Takeaways

1. **Arrays and Lists**

   o   Arrays are contiguous blocks of memory offering constant-time access by index but a fixed size.

   o   Python's list is essentially a dynamic array. It resizes automatically under the hood, balancing ease of use with strong performance.

2. **Hash Tables and Hashing**

   o   Hashing provides near O(1) lookups, insertions, and deletions on average by translating keys to indices.

o   Collision handling techniques like chaining and open addressing ensure data integrity, even if multiple keys map to the same slot.

3.   **Common Operations and Use Cases**

o   Arrays/lists shine in scenarios needing linear traversal or direct indexing.

o   Hash tables are excellent for key-based retrieval where quick lookups are paramount.

4.   **Practical Implementation**

o   You explored building your own dynamic array and hash table.

o   The dictionary application demonstrates how to integrate these data structures into a functional project.

7.2 Reflecting on the Journey

Your deep dive into arrays, lists, and hashing has covered the following:

- **Memory Layout**: Understanding how data is stored linearly and how random access is possible in arrays.

- **Pythonic Implementation**: Learning how Python's list and dict abstract away many complexities, while still benefiting from the same underlying principles.

- **Hands-On Projects**: Constructing a console-based dictionary to illustrate the real-world use of these data structures.

7.3 Moving Forward

Up next, you will expand into other fundamental data structures like **stacks, queues, and linked lists**. These will build upon the ideas covered here:

- **Stacks**: Last-In-First-Out (LIFO) containers often implemented on top of arrays or lists.

- **Queues**: First-In-First-Out (FIFO) containers, commonly used in scheduling or buffering.

- **Linked Lists**: Node-based structures that can be more efficient at insertions/deletions but less so at indexing.

Each structure offers unique advantages, and understanding them helps you decide the best tool for any problem. Remember to keep practicing—build small projects, test your code extensively, and explore how different data structures behave under stress (e.g., large inputs, frequent insertions).

Additional Resources

- *Data Structures and Algorithms in Python* by Goodrich, Tamassia, and Goldwasser.

- *Algorithms* by Robert Sedgewick and Kevin Wayne (though examples are often in Java).

- Online platforms like **LeetCode**, **HackerRank**, and **GeeksforGeeks** provide countless challenges to hone your new skills.

Encouragement

Never underestimate the value of thoroughly understanding fundamentals. Arrays, lists, and hash tables will continue to show up in nearly every programming endeavor you undertake. By mastering how they work and when to use them, you have taken a significant leap forward in your DS&A journey. Stay inquisitive and keep building— every small project is a step toward mastering more advanced topics.

Pro Tip: Keep a cheat sheet of data structure complexities—knowing the time and space complexities can quickly guide your design decisions.

CHAPTER 4: LINEAR STRUCTURES – STACKS, QUEUES, AND LINKED LISTS

I n this chapter, we delve into three fundamental linear data structures—**Stacks**, **Queues**, and **Linked Lists**—each offering unique ways to organize and manipulate data sequentially. Stacks and queues restrict how data is inserted and removed (LIFO and FIFO rules, respectively), while linked lists rely on dynamic node references rather than contiguous arrays. By mastering these structures, you'll gain powerful tools for solving a range of problems, from browser navigation to task scheduling in operating systems.

What You'll Learn

1. **Exploring Stack and Queue Structures**

    o   Definitions and conceptual overviews

    o   Classic LIFO and FIFO operations

    o   Key real-world examples (e.g., function call stacks, printer job queues)

2. **Singly vs. Doubly Linked Lists**

    o   Node-based storage models

    o   Strengths and weaknesses of each approach

    o   When linked lists are more appropriate than arrays

3. **Applications in Real-World Scenarios**

    o   Use cases for stacks (e.g., browser backtracking, undo mechanisms) o   Use cases for queues (e.g., ticketing systems, breadth-first searches)

       o   Common tasks suited for linked lists (e.g., dynamic data that frequently changes size)

4.   **Implementing Stacks, Queues, and Linked Lists in Python**

       o   Hands-on coding exercises

       o   A closer look at using lists vs. collections.deque for queues

       o   Building node-based linked list classes from scratch

5.   **Project: Designing a Browser History Manager**

       o   Integrating stacks and queues

       o   Tracking "Back" and "Forward" navigation

       o   Hands-on code for a console-based mini-application

By the end of this chapter, you will have a clear understanding of how these linear structures work, how to implement them in Python, and how they can be leveraged to build efficient, real-world applications.

1. Introduction

Modern software systems must efficiently handle sequential data in many forms—function calls, user inputs, system events, and more. Linear data structures play a pivotal role in organizing this data so it can be processed quickly and predictably.

- **Stacks** organize items according to a Last-In-First-Out (LIFO) principle, meaning the last element added is the first one retrieved. This arrangement mirrors many real-life scenarios, such as stacking plates in a cafeteria.

- **Queues** manage items on a First-In-First-Out (FIFO) basis, ensuring the earliest entry is the first processed. The classic example is a line of people waiting at a bank; the first person in line is the first served.

- **Linked Lists** store elements in nodes linked together by pointers, offering flexibility in insertion and deletion without needing contiguous memory. This can be advantageous when managing collections where frequent insertions or deletions occur in the middle of the dataset.

Why Are These Structures Important?

- **Memory Management**: Linked lists efficiently handle scenarios where items must be dynamically added or removed without significant overhead or large memory allocations.

- **Operation Efficiency**: Stacks and queues simplify logic for certain tasks (e.g., reversing data or scheduling tasks), often requiring fewer lines of code and clearer conceptual models.

- **Ubiquitous Use Cases**: From web browsers (forward/back navigation) to operating systems (process scheduling), these structures repeatedly appear in software engineering.

This chapter presents not just the theory but also step-by-step Python implementations. After exploring these fundamental concepts, you'll integrate them in a practical project — a **Browser History Manager**—which demonstrates how multiple data structures can work in tandem to deliver a seamless user experience.

2. Core Concepts and Theory

2.1 Exploring Stack Structures

A **Stack** adheres to the LIFO principle:

1. **Push**: Add a new item to the top of the stack.

2. **Pop**: Remove the most recently added item from the top.

3. **Peek**: Inspect the top item without removing it (optional but common operation).

2.1.1 Real-World Analogies

- **Plate Stack**: When you stack plates in a kitchen, the last plate you place on top is the first you take when you need a plate.

- **Undo Mechanism**: Many applications (like text editors) store recent actions in a stack so an "undo" command can pop the most recent change first.

2.1.2 Time Complexity

- **Push**: O(1) (amortized if using a Python list)

- **Pop**: O(1) (again, amortized for list)

- **Peek**: O(1)

Stacks are ideal when the addition/removal order is strictly LIFO, and you rarely need to search through all elements.

2.2 Exploring Queue Structures

A **Queue** operates on a FIFO policy:

1. **Enqueue**: Insert an element at the rear.

2. **Dequeue**: Remove the element at the front.

3. **Peek**: Examine the front element without removing it (optional).

2.2.1 Real-World Analogies

- **People Waiting in Line**: The first person in line is served first.

- **Printer Queue**: Documents are printed in the order they were submitted.

2.2.2 Time Complexity

- **Enqueue**: O(1) if using collections.deque (amortized O(1) for list, though list insertions at the front are O(n) if you do them naively).

- **Dequeue**: O(1) if using collections.deque, but O(n) for a list-based queue if you remove from the front by default.

- **Peek**: O(1)

2.3 Linked Lists

A **Linked List** is a sequence of nodes, each containing:

- **data**: The item being stored

- **pointer** (or reference) to the **next** node (in a singly linked list)

Unlike arrays/lists, linked lists do not require a contiguous block of memory. Each node can reside anywhere in memory, and nodes are connected through pointers.

2.3.1 Singly vs. Doubly Linked Lists

- **Singly Linked List**: Each node has only one pointer/reference—to the next node.

    o **Advantages**: Less memory overhead.

    o **Disadvantages**: Not efficient to traverse backwards; must rely on the head node to walk the entire list.

- **Doubly Linked List**: Each node has two pointers—one to the **next** node and one to the **previous** node.

    o **Advantages**: Easy to traverse in both directions, can remove nodes in $O(1)$ if you have direct access to them.

    o **Disadvantages**: Requires extra memory for the backward pointer.

2.3.2 Time Complexity

- **Insertion/Deletion at Head**: $O(1)$ (if you already have a reference to the head or the node to be deleted in a doubly linked list).

- **Searching**: $O(n)$ in the worst case since you must traverse the list.

- **Random Access**: $O(n)$—unlike arrays, you cannot jump directly to index i.

2.4 Applications in Real-World Scenarios

1. **Stack Applications**:

    o **Expression Evaluation** (parentheses matching, postfix expression parsing)

    o **Backtracking** (like a browser's back button)

2. **Queue Applications**:

    o **Scheduling** (CPU tasks, printing jobs)

    o **Breadth-First Search** in graph algorithms

3. **Linked List Applications**:

- o **Music Playlists**: Easy rearrangement of songs

- o **Implementation of Stacks/Queues** with minimal overhead

- o **Undo/Redo Functionality**: Forward and backward pointers in text editors

Having explored the conceptual foundations, let's move on to implementing these structures in Python, reinforcing how they operate under the hood.

3. Implementing Stacks, Queues, and Linked Lists in Python

3.1 Implementing a Stack

Although Python lists can already function as stacks using append() and pop(), let's demonstrate a lightweight Stack class to illustrate the concept more explicitly.

python

```
class Stack:

    def __init__(self):

        self.items = []


    def push(self, item):

        self.items.append(item)  # O(1) amortized

        print(f"Pushed {item} onto stack.")
```

```python
    def pop(self):
        if not self.is_empty():
            popped_item = self.items.pop()  # O(1) amortized
            print(f"Popped {popped_item} from stack.")
            return popped_item
        else:
            print("Stack is empty. Nothing to pop.")
            return None

    def peek(self):
        if not self.is_empty():
            print(f"Top item: {self.items[-1]}")
            return self.items[-1]
        else:
            print("Stack is empty.")
            return None

    def is_empty(self):
        return len(self.items) == 0

    def size(self):
        return len(self.items)

def test_stack():
```

```python
stack = Stack()

stack.push(10)

stack.push(20)

stack.push(30)

stack.peek()      # Expect 30

stack.pop()       # Removes 30

stack.peek()      # Expect 20

stack.pop()       # Removes 20

stack.pop()       # Removes 10

stack.pop()       # Stack is empty


if __name__ == "__main__":

    test_stack()
```

3.2 Implementing a Queue

Using Python's built-in collections.deque is the most efficient way to create a queue, as deque supports O(1) time complexity for appends and pops on both ends. However, we'll wrap it in a simple Queue class to keep a clear interface:

python

```python
from collections import deque


class Queue:

    def __init__(self):

        self.items = deque()
```

```python
def enqueue(self, item):
    self.items.append(item)  # O(1)
    print(f"Enqueued {item}.")


def dequeue(self):
    if not self.is_empty():
        dequeued_item = self.items.popleft()  # O(1)
        print(f"Dequeued {dequeued_item}.")
        return dequeued_item
    else:
        print("Queue is empty. Nothing to dequeue.")
        return None


def peek(self):
    if not self.is_empty():
        print(f"Front of the queue: {self.items[0]}")
        return self.items[0]
    else:
        print("Queue is empty.")
        return None


def is_empty(self):
    return len(self.items) == 0
```

```python
    def size(self):

        return len(self.items)


def test_queue():

    queue = Queue()

    queue.enqueue(1)

    queue.enqueue(2)

    queue.enqueue(3)

    queue.peek()      # Expect 1

    queue.dequeue()   # Removes 1

    queue.dequeue()   # Removes 2

    queue.dequeue()   # Removes 3

    queue.dequeue()   # Queue is empty


if __name__ == "__main__":

    test_queue()
```

3.3 Implementing a Singly Linked List

Let's create a simple node-based singly linked list. Each Node holds a value and a pointer to the next node.

python

```python
class Node:

    def __init__(self, data):
```

```python
        self.data = data
        self.next = None


class SinglyLinkedList:
    def __init__(self):
        self.head = None
        self.size = 0


    def insert_at_head(self, data):
        new_node = Node(data)
        new_node.next = self.head
        self.head = new_node
        self.size += 1
        print(f"Inserted {data} at head. Size: {self.size}")


    def insert_at_tail(self, data):
        new_node = Node(data)
        if not self.head:
            self.head = new_node
        else:
            current = self.head
            while current.next:
                current = current.next
            current.next = new_node
```

```python
        self.size += 1

        print(f"Inserted {data} at tail. Size: {self.size}")


    def delete_by_value(self, value):

        current = self.head

        prev = None


        while current:

            if current.data == value:

                if prev:

                    prev.next = current.next

                else:

                    self.head = current.next

                self.size -= 1

                print(f"Deleted {value}. Size: {self.size}")

                return

            prev = current

            current = current.next

        print(f"{value} not found in list.")


    def search(self, value):

        current = self.head

        while current:

            if current.data == value:
```

```python
            print(f"Found {value} in the list.")

            return True

        current = current.next

    print(f"{value} not found in the list.")

    return False


def display(self):

    current = self.head

    elements = []

    while current:

        elements.append(str(current.data))

        current = current.next

    print(" -> ".join(elements))


def test_singly_linked_list():

    sll = SinglyLinkedList()

    sll.insert_at_head(10)

    sll.insert_at_tail(20)

    sll.insert_at_tail(30)

    sll.display()      # 10 -> 20 -> 30

    sll.search(20)      # Found 20

    sll.delete_by_value(20)

    sll.display()      # 10 -> 30

    sll.delete_by_value(40)  # 40 not found
```

```python
if __name__ == "__main__":

    test_singly_linked_list()
```

3.4 Implementing a Doubly Linked List

Let's extend the concept to a **doubly** linked list, where each node references both the previous and next nodes. This makes deletions and certain traversals more convenient.

python

```python
class DNode:

    def __init__(self, data):

        self.data = data

        self.prev = None

        self.next = None


class DoublyLinkedList:

    def __init__(self):

        self.head = None

        self.tail = None

        self.size = 0


    def insert_at_head(self, data):

        new_node = DNode(data)

        if not self.head:

            self.head = new_node
```

```python
        self.tail = new_node
    else:
        new_node.next = self.head
        self.head.prev = new_node
        self.head = new_node
    self.size += 1
    print(f"Inserted {data} at head (DLL). Size: {self.size}")


def insert_at_tail(self, data):
    if not self.head:
        self.insert_at_head(data)
        return
    new_node = DNode(data)
    self.tail.next = new_node
    new_node.prev = self.tail
    self.tail = new_node
    self.size += 1
    print(f"Inserted {data} at tail (DLL). Size: {self.size}")


def delete_by_value(self, value):
    current = self.head
    while current:
        if current.data == value:
            if current.prev:
```

```python
                current.prev.next = current.next
            else:
                self.head = current.next
                if self.head:
                    self.head.prev = None

                if current.next:
                    current.next.prev = current.prev
                else:
                    self.tail = current.prev

                self.size -= 1
                print(f"Deleted {value} from DLL. Size: {self.size}")
                return
            current = current.next
        print(f"{value} not found in DLL.")


    def display_forward(self):
        current = self.head
        elements = []
        while current:
            elements.append(str(current.data))
            current = current.next
        print(" -> ".join(elements), "(forward)")
```

```python
def display_backward(self):
    current = self.tail
    elements = []
    while current:
        elements.append(str(current.data))
        current = current.prev
    print(" <- ".join(elements), "(backward)")


def test_doubly_linked_list():
    dll = DoublyLinkedList()
    dll.insert_at_head(10)
    dll.insert_at_tail(20)
    dll.insert_at_tail(30)
    dll.display_forward()   # 10 -> 20 -> 30
    dll.display_backward()  # 30 <- 20 <- 10
    dll.delete_by_value(20)
    dll.display_forward()   # 10 -> 30
    dll.display_backward()  # 30 <- 10


if __name__ == "__main__":
    test_doubly_linked_list()
```

These implementations give you an under-the-hood view of how lists can be managed without contiguous memory. While Python's built-in data types abstract these complexities for you, understanding node-based structures is invaluable for tackling more advanced algorithms.

4. Project: Designing a Browser History Manager

Having learned how to implement stacks, queues, and linked lists, let's combine these concepts to create a simple **Browser History Manager**. In most modern browsers, **Back** and **Forward** buttons use stacks to store navigation history:

- **Back Stack**: Holds pages that you've visited before your current page.

- **Forward Stack**: Holds pages you've navigated away from when going "back," allowing you to go "forward" again if needed.

4.1 Project Overview

Features:

1. **Visit a new page**: Clear the forward stack and push the current page onto the back stack.

2. **Back**: Pop a page from the back stack and push the current page onto the forward stack.

3. **Forward**: Pop a page from the forward stack and push the current page onto the back stack.

4. **Show current page**: Display the URL of the page you're on.

We can implement each stack using our Stack class from earlier or simply rely on Python lists. Let's take the custom approach for clarity.

4.2 Defining Our BrowserHistory Class

python

```python
class BrowserHistory:

    def __init__(self, homepage):

        # Stacks:

        self.back_stack = []

        self.forward_stack = []

        self.current_page = homepage

        print(f"Initialized browser with homepage: {self.current_page}")


    def visit(self, url):

        # Push the current page onto the back stack

        self.back_stack.append(self.current_page)

        # Navigate to the new URL

        self.current_page = url

        # Clear the forward stack

        self.forward_stack.clear()

        print(f"Visited: {url}")


    def back(self):

        if not self.back_stack:

            print("No more pages in history to go back to.")

            return

        # Push current page to forward stack

        self.forward_stack.append(self.current_page)

        # Pop from back stack to current
```

```python
        self.current_page = self.back_stack.pop()

        print(f"Moved back to: {self.current_page}")


    def forward(self):

        if not self.forward_stack:

            print("No forward history available.")

            return

        # Push current page to back stack

        self.back_stack.append(self.current_page)

        # Pop from forward stack to current

        self.current_page = self.forward_stack.pop()

        print(f"Moved forward to: {self.current_page}")


    def current(self):

        print(f"Current page: {self.current_page}")

        return self.current_page
```

4.3 Console Interface

To interact with the BrowserHistory class, let's create a simple text-based menu:

python

```python
def display_menu():

    print("\n--- Browser History Manager ---")

    print("1. Visit a new page")
```

```python
    print("2. Back")

    print("3. Forward")

    print("4. Show current page")

    print("5. Exit")


def main():

    homepage = input("Enter the homepage URL: ").strip()

    browser = BrowserHistory(homepage)


    while True:

        display_menu()

        choice = input("Select an option (1-5): ").strip()


        if choice == '1':

            url = input("Enter the new URL: ").strip()

            browser.visit(url)

        elif choice == '2':

            browser.back()

        elif choice == '3':

            browser.forward()

        elif choice == '4':

            browser.current()

        elif choice == '5':

            print("Exiting Browser History Manager.")
```

```
            break

        else:

            print("Invalid choice. Please try again.")


if __name__ == "__main__":

    main()
```

4.4 Sample Run

1. **Initialization**

csharp

Enter the homepage URL: https://www.example.com

Initialized browser with homepage: https://www.example.com

2. **Visit a New Page**

arduino

1. Visit a new page

Enter the new URL: https://www.openai.com

Visited: https://www.openai.com

3. **Back**

arduino

2. Back

Moved back to: https://www.example.com

4. **Forward**

arduino

3. Forward

Moved forward to: https://www.openai.com

5. **Show Current Page**

sql

4. Show current page

Current page: https://www.openai.com

6. **Exit**

markdown

5. Exit

Exiting Browser History Manager.

At a high level, this design harnesses two stacks to replicate how a real browser navigates through pages. While a real browser has many additional complexities (e.g., caching, secure connections, rendering engines), the essence of back-and-forward navigation is captured by these fundamental structures.

5. Troubleshooting and Problem-Solving

5.1 Common Pitfalls

1. **Index Errors with Lists**

- o Popping from an empty list (for stack or queue operations) can raise exceptions.

- o **Solution**: Always check if the list is empty before popping.

2. **Pointers in Linked Lists**

- o Forgetting to update prev or next references when deleting nodes can cause broken links or memory leaks (in lower-level languages).

- o **Solution**: Carefully handle edge cases for head and tail nodes.

3. **Off-by-One Errors**

- o When inserting or removing nodes from linked lists, it's easy to misjudge the correct position.

- o **Solution**: Thoroughly test insertion and deletion logic.

4. **Performance Concerns**

- o Using regular lists for queue operations at the front can degrade performance (O(n) for each dequeue).

- o **Solution**: Use collections.deque for efficient queue operations.

5.2 Debugging Strategies

1. **Print Statements and Visualization**

- o Print out the contents of stacks, queues, or linked lists after each operation to see exactly what changed.

2. **Step-by-Step Execution**

- o Use IDE debuggers (PyCharm, VS Code) to step through each line, especially when dealing with pointer manipulations in linked lists.

3. **Unit Tests**

- o Write test functions (test_stack(), test_queue(), test_singly_linked_list()) as we did, verifying each operation's expected result.

4. **Edge Case Testing**

o   Test scenarios like empty list insertion, removing from an empty structure, or boundary conditions (the first or last node in a linked list).

6. Advanced Techniques & Optimization

Though the straightforward implementations covered here suffice for many applications, more advanced optimizations or variations may be necessary:

1. **Priority Queues**

    o   Queues where elements have priorities, typically implemented with heaps for O(log n) insertion.

    o   Useful in scheduling tasks where higher-priority items must be processed first.

2. **Circular Queues**

    o   A queue that uses modular arithmetic to wrap around the end of an array.

    o   Improves space usage in array-based queue implementations.

3. **Linked List Variations**

    o   **Circular Linked Lists**: The last node points back to the head, enabling cyclical traversal (useful in round-robin scheduling).

    o   **Skip Lists**: Layered linked lists offering O(log n) searches by "skipping" nodes in large jumps.

4. **Memory Pooling**

    o   In high-performance systems, continuously allocating/deallocating nodes can be expensive.

    o   Specialized allocators or memory pools might be used to efficiently manage large numbers of nodes.

5. **Thread-Safe Implementations**

o   For concurrent environments (like multi-threaded applications), locks or lock-free algorithms are needed to prevent race conditions on stacks or queues.

Performance Tuning Tips

- **Minimize Copies**: For queues, prefer collections.deque to avoid costly O(n) operations from removing items at the front of a list.

- **Choose the Right Structure**: Don't shoehorn a queue where a stack is more appropriate (and vice versa).

- **Profile Your Code**: Use Python's timeit or cProfile modules to identify bottlenecks.

7. Conclusion & Next Steps

7.1 Key Takeaways

1. **Stacks**

    o   LIFO principle

    o   Excellent for undo/redo, backtracking, and nested structure parsing.

2. **Queues**

    o   FIFO principle

    o   Ideal for scheduling tasks, breadth-first traversals, and buffering.

3. **Linked Lists**

    o   Node-based, flexible structure

    o   Quick insertions/deletions at the head or tail; slower random access.

4. **Browser History Manager**

o   Showcased practical application of stack-based navigation for "Back" and "Forward" functionality.

o   Reinforced the power of combining linear data structures for real-world solutions.

7.2 Final Reflections

By working through the theory and Python implementations, you've solidified your understanding of how linear structures operate and how to integrate them into cohesive applications. These structures underscore a variety of everyday problems, from the simplest console application to complex, multi-threaded systems.

Next Steps

- **Explore Non-Linear Data Structures**: Trees, graphs, and heaps open the door to advanced search, sorting, and pathfinding algorithms.

- **Continue Building Projects**: Extend your browser history manager or create new projects that utilize stacks, queues, or linked lists (e.g., a text editor with undo/redo, a round-robin scheduler simulation).

- **Enhance Your Repertoire**: Experiment with priority queues, circular linked lists, or skip lists to address specialized performance needs.

Additional Resources

- *Data Structures and Algorithms in Python* by Goodrich, Tamassia, and Goldwasser.

- Online coding platforms like **LeetCode** and **HackerRank** for practicing stack/queue/linked list problems.

With linear structures under your belt, you're ready to transition to **Trees**, **Graphs**, and other more intricate structures. Keep practicing, keep coding, and let these fundamental principles guide your design choices in all your future software endeavors!

CHAPTER 5:
HIERARCHICAL STRUCTURES – TREES AND BINARY TREES

T rees are an integral part of computer science, providing hierarchical data organization that facilitates efficient searching, insertion, and various other operations. This chapter explores the foundational concepts of **trees, binary trees**, and **binary search trees (BSTs)**. You will learn about different types of trees, their real-world applications, and how to traverse them in multiple ways. We will also walk through a hands-on project where you build a **File System Explorer**—a simplified model of an operating system's directory structure—using a tree-like data representation.

Topics Covered:

1. **Introduction to Trees and Their Types**

   o Tree fundamentals and terminology (root, children, leaves, height, depth)

   o Variations such as general trees, binary trees, and specialized trees (e.g., AVL, Red-Black)

2. **Binary Trees and Binary Search Trees**

   o Binary Tree structure

   o Binary Search Tree properties (ordered data)

   o Common BST operations (search, insert, delete)

3. **Traversal Techniques (In-order, Pre-order, Post-order)**

   o Definitions and use cases

   o Implementation strategies for each traversal method

4. **Implementing Trees in Python**

   o   Node-based classes

   o   Recursive algorithms for traversal

   o   Building a basic binary search tree

5. **Project: Building a File System Explorer**

   o   Conceptualizing a hierarchical folder-and-file structure

   o   Using tree data structures to represent directories and files

   o   A console-based application to navigate, list, and manage file-system-like nodes

By the end of this chapter, you'll be well-equipped to handle hierarchical data structures, design efficient traversal algorithms, and utilize trees in practical applications.

1. Introduction to Trees and Their Types

1.1 Tree Fundamentals

A **tree** is a hierarchical data structure composed of nodes connected by edges. Each node can have zero or more children, and there is exactly one path between any two nodes. Trees offer a way to model real-world hierarchies (e.g., file systems, organizational charts) and often allow faster searching and insertion compared to linear structures if balanced properly.

Key Terminology:

- **Root**: The topmost node of the tree.

- **Child**: A node immediately below another node.

- **Parent**: A node that has one or more child nodes.

- **Leaf**: A node with no children.

- **Height**: The maximum level of depth in a tree. A leaf has height 0; the height of a non-leaf node is 1 + the height of its deepest child.

- **Depth**: The level of a node relative to the root, typically starting at 0 for the root.

1.2 Types of Trees

1. **General Tree**: A node can have any number of children.

2. **Binary Tree**: A node can have at most two children, often referred to as left and right.

3. **Binary Search Tree (BST)**: A binary tree with the property that left descendants contain values less than (or equal to) the node's value, and right descendants contain values greater than the node's value.

Other specialized trees include **heaps**, **AVL trees**, **Red-Black trees**, and **B-Trees**, which offer specific guarantees like balanced height or efficient disk access. This chapter focuses on the core principles of general trees and binary trees, setting a foundation for understanding these more advanced variants.

2. Binary Trees and Binary Search Trees

2.1 Binary Trees

A **binary tree** limits each node to two children (left and right). Even with this constraint, binary trees can represent a wide range of hierarchical data. They underpin many algorithms and data structures, including expression trees, decision trees, and heaps.

Key Properties:

- Maximum of 2 children per node.

- Potential for multiple shapes even with the same input data.

- Commonly used for parsing (like expression trees) and traversal-based operations.

2.2 Binary Search Trees (BSTs)

A **binary search tree** adds an ordering constraint:

1. **Left Subtree**: Contains nodes with values less than (or equal to) the current node's value.

2. **Right Subtree**: Contains nodes with values greater than the current node's value.

3. **No Duplicate Nodes** (commonly, though some BST variants allow duplicates in the left or right subtree).

BST Operations and Time Complexities (Average Case):

- **Search**: O(log n)

- **Insert**: O(log n)

- **Delete**: O(log n)

If the tree becomes skewed (like a linked list), these operations degrade to O(n). Balanced BSTs (e.g., AVL, Red-Black) ensure more consistent log-time performance.

2.3 BST Use Cases

1. **Databases**: Storing sorted data or maintaining indexes.

2. **Compiler Syntax Trees**: Representing expressions in a structured format.

3. **File Systems** (though they often use more advanced tree-like structures like B-trees).

3. Traversal Techniques (In-order, Pre-order, Post-order)

Tree traversal is how you visit each node in a tree. Traversals are crucial for data processing—whether you want to print, search, or process each node in a specific order.

3.1 In-order Traversal

Definition: Traverse left subtree, visit the root, then traverse right subtree.
Pseudocode:

scss

```
inorder(node):

    if node is not null:

        inorder(node.left)

        visit(node)

        inorder(node.right)
```

Use Case: Retrieving data from a BST in sorted (ascending) order.

3.2 Pre-order Traversal

Definition: Visit the root first, then traverse left subtree, then traverse right subtree.
Pseudocode:

scss

```
preorder(node):
```

```
if node is not null:

    visit(node)

    preorder(node.left)

    preorder(node.right)
```

Use Case: ing a tree structure, building expression strings, or serializing a tree.

3.3 Post-order Traversal

Definition: Traverse left subtree, traverse right subtree, then visit the root.
Pseudocode:

scss

```
postorder(node):

    if node is not null:

        postorder(node.left)

        postorder(node.right)

        visit(node)
```

Use Case: Deleting all nodes in a tree (freeing memory in lower-level languages), or evaluating expression trees (visit children before applying operator at the root).

4. Implementing Trees in Python

4.1 Generic Tree Node

Let's start by implementing a simple node class for a general (multi-child) tree structure:

python

```python
class TreeNode:

    def __init__(self, value):

        self.value = value

        self.children = []  # can hold multiple children


    def add_child(self, child):

        self.children.append(child)


    def remove_child(self, child):

        self.children = [c for c in self.children if c != child]
```

Usage: This generic structure might be enough for certain hierarchical data like directories and subdirectories.

4.2 Binary Tree Node

python

```python
class BinaryTreeNode:

    def __init__(self, value):

        self.value = value

        self.left = None

        self.right = None
```

4.3 Binary Search Tree Implementation

python

```python
class BinarySearchTree:

    def __init__(self):

        self.root = None


    def insert(self, value):

        if self.root is None:

            self.root = BinaryTreeNode(value)

        else:

            self._insert_recursive(self.root, value)


    def _insert_recursive(self, current_node, value):

        if value < current_node.value:

            if current_node.left is None:

                current_node.left = BinaryTreeNode(value)

            else:

                self._insert_recursive(current_node.left, value)

        else:

            if current_node.right is None:

                current_node.right = BinaryTreeNode(value)

            else:

                self._insert_recursive(current_node.right, value)


    def search(self, value):

        return self._search_recursive(self.root, value)
```

```python
def _search_recursive(self, current_node, value):

    if current_node is None:

        return False

    if value == current_node.value:

        return True

    elif value < current_node.value:

        return self._search_recursive(current_node.left, value)

    else:

        return self._search_recursive(current_node.right, value)


def inorder(self):

    self._inorder_recursive(self.root)

    print()  # new line after traversal


def _inorder_recursive(self, node):

    if node is not None:

        self._inorder_recursive(node.left)

        print(node.value, end=' ')

        self._inorder_recursive(node.right)


def preorder(self):

    self._preorder_recursive(self.root)

    print()
```

```python
def _preorder_recursive(self, node):

    if node is not None:

        print(node.value, end=' ')

        self._preorder_recursive(node.left)

        self._preorder_recursive(node.right)


def postorder(self):

    self._postorder_recursive(self.root)

    print()


def _postorder_recursive(self, node):

    if node is not None:

        self._postorder_recursive(node.left)

        self._postorder_recursive(node.right)

        print(node.value, end=' ')
```

4.3.1 Testing the BST

python

```python
def test_bst():

    bst = BinarySearchTree()

    values_to_insert = [10, 5, 15, 2, 7, 12, 20]

    for val in values_to_insert:

        bst.insert(val)
```

```python
# Search tests

print("Searching for 7:", bst.search(7))   # True

print("Searching for 99:", bst.search(99)) # False


# Traversal tests

print("In-order traversal (should be sorted):")

bst.inorder()

print("Pre-order traversal:")

bst.preorder()

print("Post-order traversal:")

bst.postorder()


if __name__ == "__main__":

    test_bst()
```

Sample Output:

yaml

```
Searching for 7: True

Searching for 99: False

In-order traversal (should be sorted):

2 5 7 10 12 15 20

Pre-order traversal:

10 5 2 7 15 12 20
```

Post-order traversal:

2 7 5 12 20 15 10

5. Project: Building a File System Explorer

Now let's create a console-based **File System Explorer** to manage a simple directory tree. Each node can represent either a folder or a file. Folders act like tree nodes with children, whereas files can be leaf nodes.

5.1 Project Overview

Features:

1. **Navigation**: Move up or down the directory tree.

2. **Listing Contents**: Display all items (subdirectories/files) in the current folder.

3. **Add/Remove Items**: Create or delete files/folders in the current directory.

While real file systems have many complexities (permissions, disk storage, etc.), this project focuses on the tree-structured relationships.

5.2 Designing the Data Structure

python

```
class FSNode:

    def __init__(self, name, is_file=False):

        self.name = name

        self.is_file = is_file

        self.children = []  # only valid if is_file == False
```

```python
def add_child(self, child_node):

    if self.is_file:

        print(f"Cannot add child to file: {self.name}")

        return

    self.children.append(child_node)


def remove_child(self, child_name):

    if self.is_file:

        print(f"Cannot remove child from file: {self.name}")

        return

    self.children = [child for child in self.children if child.name != child_name]
```

1. **name**: The folder or file name.

2. **is_file**: Boolean indicating whether it's a file or folder.

3. **children**: List of FSNodes (subdirectories or files). Only valid when is_file is False.

5.3 Building a Sample File System

python

```python
def build_sample_fs():

    root = FSNode("root", is_file=False)


    # Create folders

    documents = FSNode("Documents", False)
```

```python
pictures = FSNode("Pictures", False)

music = FSNode("Music", False)

root.add_child(documents)

root.add_child(pictures)

root.add_child(music)


# Create files in Documents

doc1 = FSNode("resume.pdf", True)

doc2 = FSNode("cover_letter.docx", True)

documents.add_child(doc1)

documents.add_child(doc2)


# Create a subfolder in Pictures

vacation_photos = FSNode("Vacation", False)

pictures.add_child(vacation_photos)

vac1 = FSNode("beach.png", True)

vac2 = FSNode("mountains.jpg", True)

vacation_photos.add_child(vac1)

vacation_photos.add_child(vac2)


# Create files in Music

track1 = FSNode("song.mp3", True)

track2 = FSNode("theme.wav", True)

music.add_child(track1)
```

```
music.add_child(track2)


return root
```

5.4 Implementing the Explorer Interface

python

```python
class FileSystemExplorer:

    def __init__(self, root):

        self.root = root

        self.current_node = root

        self.path_stack = []  # to track navigation


    def list_contents(self):

        if self.current_node.is_file:

            print(f"{self.current_node.name} is a file.")

        else:

            if not self.current_node.children:

                print("No contents.")

                return

            for child in self.current_node.children:

                file_or_folder = "File" if child.is_file else "Folder"

                print(f"{child.name} - {file_or_folder}")
```

```python
def change_directory(self, name):

    if self.current_node.is_file:

        print("Cannot cd into a file.")

        return

    if name == "..":

        # Move up one directory if possible

        if self.path_stack:

            self.current_node = self.path_stack.pop()

        else:

            print("Already at the root directory.")

        return

    # Move down into a child

    for child in self.current_node.children:

        if child.name == name and not child.is_file:

            self.path_stack.append(self.current_node)

            self.current_node = child

            return

    print(f"Directory '{name}' not found or is a file.")


def make_directory(self, name):

    if self.current_node.is_file:

        print("Cannot create directory in a file.")

        return

    new_dir = FSNode(name, False)
```

```python
        self.current_node.add_child(new_dir)

        print(f"Folder '{name}' created.")


    def create_file(self, name):
        if self.current_node.is_file:

            print("Cannot create file inside another file.")

            return

        new_file = FSNode(name, True)

        self.current_node.add_child(new_file)

        print(f"File '{name}' created.")


    def delete_item(self, name):
        if self.current_node.is_file:

            print("Cannot delete items within a file.")

            return

        self.current_node.remove_child(name)

        print(f"Item '{name}' deleted.")


    def current_path(self):
        path_names = [node.name for node in self.path_stack] + [self.current_node.name]

        path_str = "/".join(path_names)

        print(f"Current path: /{path_str}" if path_str else "/")


def main():
```

```python
root = build_sample_fs()

explorer = FileSystemExplorer(root)


while True:

    explorer.current_path()

    command = input("Enter command (ls, cd <dir>, mkdir <name>, touch <file>, rm <name>, quit): ").strip()


    if command == "ls":

        explorer.list_contents()

    elif command.startswith("cd"):

        _, dir_name = command.split(maxsplit=1)

        explorer.change_directory(dir_name)

    elif command.startswith("mkdir"):

        _, folder_name = command.split(maxsplit=1)

        explorer.make_directory(folder_name)

    elif command.startswith("touch"):

        _, file_name = command.split(maxsplit=1)

        explorer.create_file(file_name)

    elif command.startswith("rm"):

        _, item_name = command.split(maxsplit=1)

        explorer.delete_item(item_name)

    elif command == "quit":

        print("Exiting File System Explorer.")
```

```python
            break

        else:

            print("Unknown command.")


if __name__ == "__main__":

    main()
```

5.5 Sample Interaction

bash

Current path: /root

Enter command (ls, cd <dir>, mkdir <name>, touch <file>, rm <name>, quit): ls

Documents - Folder

Pictures - Folder

Music - Folder

Current path: /root

Enter command: cd Documents

Current path: /root/Documents

Enter command: ls

resume.pdf - File

cover_letter.docx - File

Current path: /root/Documents

Enter command: touch project_plan.docx

File 'project_plan.docx' created.

Current path: /root/Documents

Enter command: ls

resume.pdf - File

cover_letter.docx - File

project_plan.docx - File

Current path: /root/Documents

Enter command: cd ..

Current path: /root

Enter command: quit

Exiting File System Explorer.

Project Notes:

- This simple file explorer uses a tree-like structure (with possible multiple children).

- Navigation is implemented using a stack (path_stack) to store the history of traversed directories, enabling you to go "up" a level easily.

- Creating and deleting files or folders manipulates the children of the current node, illustrating how trees can dynamically grow or shrink.

6. Troubleshooting and Problem-Solving

6.1 Common Pitfalls

1. **Null References**: Failing to check if node is None before recursing (e.g., in BST insertions or search).

2. **Skewed BSTs**: Inserting already-sorted data can create a linear chain, hurting performance (O(n)).

3. **Traversals**: Mixing up left and right traversal calls can yield incorrect results.

4. **File System Loops**: In a real OS, symbolic links or special references can create cycles; a pure tree model must be careful to avoid infinite loops.

6.2 Debugging Tips

1. **Print Intermediate States**: Show subtree during insertions or deletions (especially for BST).

2. **Visual Representation**: Sketching the tree structure helps clarify parent-child relationships.

3. **Unit Testing**: Write targeted tests for critical methods (insert, search, delete).

4. **Edge Cases**: Test empty trees, single-node trees, or removal of the root in BST.

6.3 Performance Considerations

- **Balancing**: Consider self-balancing trees (AVL, Red-Black) for large-scale applications.

- **Memory Usage**: Each node carries references (like left, right, children), which might be overhead if large arrays suffice.

- **Concurrency**: Locking or transactional memory is needed if multiple threads modify a tree simultaneously.

7. Conclusion & Next Steps

7.1 Key Takeaways

1. **Tree Concepts**

   o Trees model hierarchical data and support recursive operations.

   o Binary trees constrain each node to two children.

   o Binary search trees enforce an ordering that speeds up searches and inserts (average-case O(log n)).

2. **Traversal Methods**

   o **In-order**: Perfect for sorted data retrieval in BSTs.

   o **Pre-order**: Useful for replicating tree structure or expression evaluation.

   o **Post-order**: Often employed in deleting or evaluating child nodes first.

3. **Practical Implementation**

   o You learned to implement node-based trees, BST operations, and traversal algorithms in Python.

   o The **File System Explorer** demonstrated how tree structures model real-world hierarchies dynamically.

7.2 Reflect on Your Progress

Understanding trees paves the way for mastering more complex data structures and algorithms. Many advanced structures—like **heaps**, **tries**, and **segment trees**—build on the principles you've just learned.

7.3 Next Steps

Upcoming Topics:

- **Graph Data Structures**: Extend beyond trees to represent interconnected data (where cycles may exist).

- **Advanced Tree Variants**: Balanced BSTs, tries for prefix-based searching, and more.

- **Algorithmic Challenges**: Practice tree problems on platforms like LeetCode or HackerRank.

7.4 Additional Resources

- *Data Structures and Algorithms in Python* by Goodrich, Tamassia, and Goldwasser.

- *Introduction to Algorithms* by Cormen, Leiserson, Rivest, and Stein (for more advanced tree structures).

- Online tutorials (GeeksforGeeks, Educative) for advanced tree and graph concepts.

Final Encouragement

By building a file explorer, you have a hands-on example of how tree-based structures can be integrated into real-life applications. Keep experimenting—perhaps add a move command or implement search functionality in your file explorer. This practice will strengthen your grasp of how trees function in software systems. Onwards to exploring graphs and more complex data structures!

CHAPTER 6: GRAPHS AND GRAPH ALGORITHMS

G raphs model relationships between entities (nodes or vertices) through connections called edges. They are central to various real-world problems: from social networks and transportation routes to recommendation engines and search algorithms. This chapter covers the fundamentals of **graphs and their components**, explores **common graph algorithms** such as **Breadth-First Search (BFS)**, **Depth-First Search (DFS)**, and **Dijkstra's algorithm**, then shows you how to implement graphs and these algorithms in Python. You will also build a **Social Network Connection Finder** as a practical project to illustrate how graph operations can unearth meaningful insights (like shortest paths or connectivity) in your data.

1. Understanding Graphs and Their Components

1.1 Graph Definition

A **graph** GGG is a set of **vertices** (or **nodes**) and a collection of **edges** (connections between pairs of vertices). Formally:

$G=(V,E)G = (V, E)G=(V,E)$

- VVV is the set of vertices.

- EEE is the set of edges, where each edge links two vertices.

1.2 Graph Terminology

1. **Vertex (Node)**: A point in the graph (e.g., a user in a social network).

2. **Edge**: A connection between two vertices. Edges can be **directed** or **undirected**.

3. **Adjacent Vertices (Neighbors)**: Vertices connected directly by an edge.

4. **Degree**: The number of edges incident to a vertex. In a directed graph, there are in-degrees and out-degrees.

5. **Path**: A sequence of edges connecting a sequence of distinct vertices.

6. **Cycle**: A path starting and ending at the same vertex without repeating edges or vertices (other than the start/end).

7. **Connected (Undirected Graph)**: A graph is connected if there is a path between every pair of vertices.

1.3 Types of Graphs

1. **Undirected Graph**: Edges have no direction; an edge (u,v) is the same as (v,u).

2. **Directed Graph (Digraph)**: Edges have directions; (u,v) and (v,u) are distinct, representing possible one-way relationships.

3. **Weighted Graph**: Each edge has an associated weight (cost or distance), commonly used in route-finding (maps, networks).

4. **Unweighted Graph**: Edges have no particular cost. BFS is often used for shortest path in such graphs.

Real-World Examples:

- **Social Networks**: People (nodes) connected by friendships/follows (edges).

- **Road Maps**: Cities (nodes) connected by roads (edges), often with distances or travel times (weights).

- **Computer Networks**: Routers (nodes) connected by links (edges) with bandwidth or latency (weights).

2. Common Graph Algorithms

2.1 Breadth-First Search (BFS)

Purpose: Traverse or search in a graph (or tree) level by level. Particularly useful for finding the shortest path in an **unweighted** graph (in terms of number of edges).

Key Steps:

1.   Start at a **source** vertex.

2.   Visit all neighbors of the source, then move on to the neighbors of those neighbors, and so on.

3.   Use a **queue** to manage vertices to explore.

Time Complexity: $O(V+E)O(V + E)O(V+E)$ for a graph with VVV vertices and EEE edges.

Pseudocode:

less

```
BFS(graph, start):

    create a queue Q

    mark start as visited

    enqueue start into Q


    while Q is not empty:

      vertex = dequeue Q

      for neighbor in graph[vertex]:

        if neighbor not visited:

          mark neighbor as visited

          enqueue neighbor
```

2.2 Depth-First Search (DFS)

Purpose: Traverse or search in a graph by exploring as far as possible along each branch before backtracking. Useful for tasks like detecting cycles, topological sorting, or connectivity.

Key Steps:

1. Start at a **source** vertex.

2. Recursively explore one branch fully before moving to the next branch.

3. Use a **stack** (implicitly via recursion or explicitly) to track the exploration path.

Time Complexity: $O(V+E)O(V + E)O(V+E)$.

Recursive Pseudocode:

scss

```
DFS(graph, start):

    mark start as visited

    for neighbor in graph[start]:

        if neighbor not visited:

            DFS(graph, neighbor)
```

2.3 Dijkstra's Algorithm

Purpose: Finds the **shortest path** from a source vertex to all other vertices in a **weighted** graph with **non-negative** edge weights.

Key Steps:

1. Initialize distances of all vertices to infinity, except the start vertex set to 0.

2. Use a **priority queue** to pick the next closest vertex.

3. Update distances to neighbors of the chosen vertex if a shorter path is found.

4. Repeat until all reachable vertices are processed.

Time Complexity:

- Using a **binary heap** (priority queue): $O((V+E)\log V)O((V + E) \log V)O((V+E)\log V)$.

Pseudocode (simplified):

less

```
Dijkstra(graph, source):
  dist[source] = 0
  for vertex in graph:
    if vertex != source:
      dist[vertex] = infinity
  create a min-priority-queue Q of all vertices with key=dist[vertex]


  while Q is not empty:
    u = extract-min(Q)
    for neighbor v of u:
      if dist[u] + weight(u, v) < dist[v]:
        dist[v] = dist[u] + weight(u, v)
        decrease-key(Q, v, dist[v])
```

3. Implementing Graphs in Python

3.1 Graph Representation

1. **Adjacency List**: A dictionary or list of lists, where each key or index represents a vertex and stores a list of adjacent vertices.

    o   **Pros**: Space-efficient for sparse graphs.

    o   **Cons**: Finding if an edge exists between two arbitrary vertices can take $O(deg(v))$ time.

2. **Adjacency Matrix**: A 2D matrix where element $(i,j)(i, j)(i,j)$ is 1 (or weight) if there is an edge from iii to jjj.

    o   **Pros**: Quick edge existence check.

    o   **Cons**: Potentially large space usage ($O(V2)O(V^2)O(V2)$), inefficient for sparse graphs.

In Python, adjacency lists are commonly used due to their flexibility and efficiency for sparse graphs.

3.2 Building a Graph Class

python

```
class Graph:

    def __init__(self, directed=False):

        self.adjacency_list = {}

        self.directed = directed


    def add_vertex(self, vertex):

        if vertex not in self.adjacency_list:
```

```python
        self.adjacency_list[vertex] = []


    def add_edge(self, u, v, weight=1):
        # Ensure both vertices exist in the graph
        if u not in self.adjacency_list:
            self.add_vertex(u)
        if v not in self.adjacency_list:
            self.add_vertex(v)


        # Add an edge from u to v
        self.adjacency_list[u].append((v, weight))


        # If undirected, add an edge from v to u
        if not self.directed:
            self.adjacency_list[v].append((u, weight))


    def get_vertices(self):
        return list(self.adjacency_list.keys())


    def get_edges(self):
        edges = []
        for u in self.adjacency_list:
            for (v, w) in self.adjacency_list[u]:
                if self.directed:
```

```python
            edges.append((u, v, w))
        else:
            # For undirected, ensure each edge is listed once
            if (v, u, w) not in edges:
                edges.append((u, v, w))
    return edges


def display(self):
    for vertex in self.adjacency_list:
        print(f"{vertex} -> {self.adjacency_list[vertex]}")


def test_graph():
    g = Graph(directed=False)
    g.add_edge("A", "B")
    g.add_edge("A", "C", 2)
    g.add_edge("B", "D", 3)
    g.add_edge("C", "D", 1)
    g.display()


if __name__ == "__main__":
    test_graph()
```

Sample Output:

css

A -> [('B', 1), ('C', 2)]

B -> [('A', 1), ('D', 3)]

C -> [('A', 2), ('D', 1)]

D -> [('B', 3), ('C', 1)]

4. Project: Developing a Social Network Connection Finder

4.1 Project Overview

Goal: Build a simple console-based application to discover shortest paths and friend suggestions in a social network.

- **Nodes**: People (identified by unique names or IDs).

- **Edges**: Friend relationships (unweighted, undirected).

- **Queries**:

    1. Check if two people are directly connected.

    2. Find the shortest path (in terms of number of friendships) between two people.

    3. Suggest new friends based on mutual connections (optional advanced feature).

4.2 Data Model

We'll use the **Graph** class from above. Each vertex is a person's name, and edges represent friendships.

4.3 Core Features

1. **Add Person**: Insert a new person (vertex) into the network.

2. **Add Friendship**: Add an undirected edge between two people.

3. **Check Connection**: Use BFS (or DFS) to see if two people are connected (i.e., if there is a path).

4. **Find Shortest Path**: Use BFS to find the shortest path in an unweighted graph.

5. **Suggest Friends** (Optional): Based on shared connections.

4.4 BFS for Shortest Path

We'll modify BFS slightly to track the path from a **start** to a **target**. When we enqueue a neighbor, we store its "parent" (the node from which we reached it). Once we find the target, we backtrack using these parents to reconstruct the path.

Modified BFS:

python

```python
def bfs_shortest_path(graph, start, target):

    from collections import deque


    visited = set()

    parent = {}  # map each node to its parent in the BFS tree


    queue = deque([start])

    visited.add(start)

    parent[start] = None  # no parent for start
```

```python
    while queue:

        current = queue.popleft()

        if current == target:

            # reconstruct path

            return build_path(parent, start, target)


        for (neighbor, _) in graph.adjacency_list[current]:

            if neighbor not in visited:

                visited.add(neighbor)

                parent[neighbor] = current

                queue.append(neighbor)


    return None  # target not found


def build_path(parent, start, target):

    path = []

    current = target

    while current is not None:

        path.append(current)

        current = parent[current]

    path.reverse()

    return path
```

4.5 Implementing the Connection Finder

python

```python
class SocialNetwork:

    def __init__(self):

        self.graph = Graph(directed=False)


    def add_person(self, person):

        self.graph.add_vertex(person)

        print(f"Added person '{person}' to the network.")


    def add_friendship(self, p1, p2):

        self.graph.add_edge(p1, p2, weight=1)

        print(f"Added friendship between '{p1}' and '{p2}'.")


    def check_connection(self, p1, p2):

        # Simple BFS or DFS to see if there's a path

        path = bfs_shortest_path(self.graph, p1, p2)

        if path:

            print(f"'{p1}' and '{p2}' are connected via {path}")

        else:

            print(f"No connection found between '{p1}' and '{p2}'.")


    def find_shortest_path(self, p1, p2):
```

```python
        path = bfs_shortest_path(self.graph, p1, p2)

        if path:

            print(f"Shortest path between '{p1}' and '{p2}': {' -> '.join(path)}")

        else:

            print(f"No path exists between '{p1}' and '{p2}'.")


    # Optional: A feature to suggest new friends

    def suggest_friends(self, person):

        if person not in self.graph.adjacency_list:

            print(f"Person '{person}' does not exist.")

            return


        # For each neighbor of 'person', gather their neighbors

        # Exclude 'person' itself and direct friends

        direct_friends = set([nbr for (nbr, _) in self.graph.adjacency_list[person]])

        suggestions = {}

        for (friend, _) in self.graph.adjacency_list[person]:

            for (friend_of_friend, _) in self.graph.adjacency_list[friend]:

                # Skip if it's the person or already a direct friend

                if friend_of_friend == person or friend_of_friend in direct_friends:

                    continue

                suggestions[friend_of_friend] = suggestions.get(friend_of_friend, 0) + 1


        # Sort suggestions by highest number of mutual friends
```

```python
        sorted_suggestions = sorted(suggestions.items(), key=lambda x: x[1], reverse=True)
        if sorted_suggestions:
            print("Friend suggestions for '{}':".format(person))
            for (suggested_person, mutual_count) in sorted_suggestions:
                print(f"{suggested_person} (mutual friends: {mutual_count})")
        else:
            print(f"No new friend suggestions for '{person}'.")


def main():
    network = SocialNetwork()
    while True:
        print("\nSocial Network Connection Finder")
        print("1. Add Person")
        print("2. Add Friendship")
        print("3. Check Connection")
        print("4. Find Shortest Path")
        print("5. Suggest Friends (Optional)")
        print("6. Exit")
        choice = input("Enter choice (1-6): ")


        if choice == '1':
            name = input("Enter person's name: ").strip()
            network.add_person(name)
        elif choice == '2':
```

```python
        p1 = input("Enter first person's name: ").strip()

        p2 = input("Enter second person's name: ").strip()

        network.add_friendship(p1, p2)

    elif choice == '3':

        p1 = input("Enter first person's name: ").strip()

        p2 = input("Enter second person's name: ").strip()

        network.check_connection(p1, p2)

    elif choice == '4':

        p1 = input("Enter start person's name: ").strip()

        p2 = input("Enter target person's name: ").strip()

        network.find_shortest_path(p1, p2)

    elif choice == '5':

        person = input("Enter person's name: ").strip()

        network.suggest_friends(person)

    elif choice == '6':

        print("Exiting Social Network Connection Finder.")

        break

    else:

        print("Invalid choice. Try again.")


if __name__ == "__main__":

    main()
```

4.6 Sample Interaction

rust

Social Network Connection Finder

1. Add Person

2. Add Friendship

3. Check Connection

4. Find Shortest Path

5. Suggest Friends (Optional)

6. Exit

Enter choice (1-6): 1

Enter person's name: Alice

Added person 'Alice' to the network.

Social Network Connection Finder

...

Enter choice (1-6): 1

Enter person's name: Bob

Added person 'Bob' to the network.

Social Network Connection Finder

...

Enter choice (1-6): 2

Enter first person's name: Alice

Enter second person's name: Bob

Added friendship between 'Alice' and 'Bob'.

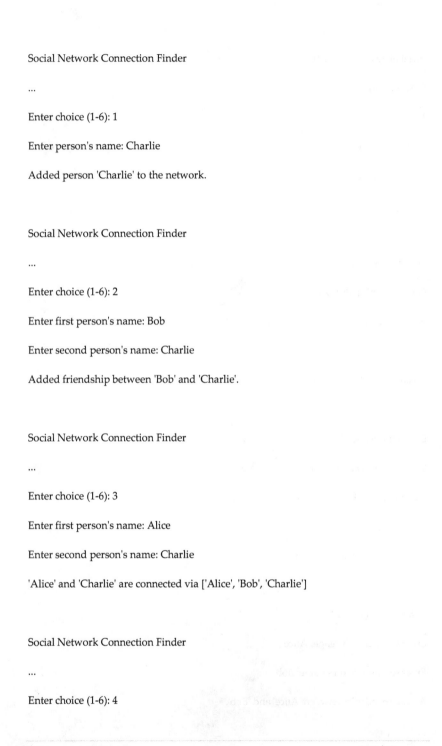

Social Network Connection Finder

...

Enter choice (1-6): 1

Enter person's name: Charlie

Added person 'Charlie' to the network.

Social Network Connection Finder

...

Enter choice (1-6): 2

Enter first person's name: Bob

Enter second person's name: Charlie

Added friendship between 'Bob' and 'Charlie'.

Social Network Connection Finder

...

Enter choice (1-6): 3

Enter first person's name: Alice

Enter second person's name: Charlie

'Alice' and 'Charlie' are connected via ['Alice', 'Bob', 'Charlie']

Social Network Connection Finder

...

Enter choice (1-6): 4

Enter start person's name: Alice

Enter target person's name: Charlie

Shortest path between 'Alice' and 'Charlie': Alice -> Bob -> Charlie

...

Enter choice (1-6): 6

Exiting Social Network Connection Finder.

Explanation:

- We added **Alice, Bob, Charlie** as people.

- **Alice** and **Bob** are friends; **Bob** and **Charlie** are friends.

- Checking connection or the shortest path from **Alice** to **Charlie** yields the path **[Alice -> Bob -> Charlie]**.

5. Troubleshooting and Problem-Solving

5.1 Common Pitfalls

1. **Unvisited vs. Visited State**: Failing to track visited nodes can cause infinite loops, especially in cyclic graphs.

2. **Directed vs. Undirected**: Mixing them up can produce incorrect traversal or pathfinding results.

3. **Edge Cases**: Non-existent vertices, adding duplicate edges, or searching from a node that isn't in the graph.

4. **Large Graph Performance**: BFS/DFS is O(V+E)O(V + E)O(V+E), but Dijkstra can become expensive if not using a proper priority queue or if the graph is very dense.

5.2 Debugging Tips

1. **Visual Representation**: Sketch the graph or use a graph-drawing tool.

2. **Print Statements**: After each insertion or search step, print partial results (like visited sets, current queue/stack state).

3. **Unit Tests**: For BFS, DFS, Dijkstra, test small graphs with known outcomes (including disconnected graphs or ones with cycles).

4. **Check for Off-by-One Errors**: Particularly in adjacency matrix indexing; less common with adjacency lists, but still watchful if using numeric IDs.

5.3 Performance Considerations

- **Sparse vs. Dense Graph**: Adjacency lists are often better for sparse graphs (few edges relative to $V2V^2V2$).

- **Priority Queues**: Efficiently implement Dijkstra's with a binary heap or a Fibonacci heap for large graphs.

- **Parallelization**: BFS can be parallelized on certain architectures (e.g., large-scale graph processing in HPC).

6. Advanced Techniques & Optimization

After learning the basic graph algorithms, consider the following expansions:

1. **Topological Sort**: For directed acyclic graphs (DAGs), order the vertices such that all directed edges go from a preceding vertex to a subsequent vertex (common in dependency management).

2. **Minimum Spanning Tree (MST)**: Algorithms like **Kruskal** or **Prim** to find the tree connecting all vertices with the minimal total edge weight.

3. **A***: A pathfinding algorithm using heuristics, often used in game development and navigation systems.

4. **Bellman-Ford, Floyd-Warshall**: Shortest path algorithms accommodating negative edge weights.

Optimizations:

- **Pruning**: In BFS or DFS, skip branches when unnecessary (depending on problem constraints).

- **Heuristics** (A*): Speeds up search with domain knowledge.

- **Disjoint Set (Union-Find)**: Efficient structure for checking connected components or cycles in undirected graphs.

7. Conclusion & Next Steps

7.1 Key Takeaways

1. **Graph Fundamentals**

   o Vertices and edges model connections in various domains (social networks, maps, networks).

   o Graphs can be directed or undirected, weighted or unweighted.

2. **Core Algorithms**

   o **BFS**: Level-by-level exploration, ideal for shortest path in an unweighted graph.

   o **DFS**: Depth-based exploration, useful for cycle detection, connectivity, or topological sort.

   o **Dijkstra's**: Shortest path in non-negative, weighted graphs.

3. **Practical Implementations**

   o You built a Graph class in Python using adjacency lists.

   o Demonstrated BFS for shortest paths, DFS for deep search, and Dijkstra's for weighted shortest paths (the latter in concept; can be implemented similarly).

o   A real-world **Social Network Connection Finder** project combined these ideas.

7.2 Reflect on Your Journey

By integrating BFS into a real-world context (social networks), you've seen how theoretical graph concepts translate into tangible, user-facing features. This approach is generalizable: any domain where items relate to each other can be mapped onto a graph, and algorithms like BFS, DFS, and Dijkstra's can uncover valuable information.

7.3 Next Steps

1. **Explore Advanced Graph Algorithms**: Minimum Spanning Trees (Kruskal's, Prim's), maximum flow (Ford-Fulkerson), topological sorts, etc.

2. **Work with Larger Datasets**: Load data from files or APIs (e.g., real social network data) to test performance.

3. **Enhance the Connection Finder**: Incorporate weighting, more complex queries, or advanced pathfinding.

4. **Look Ahead to More Complex DS&A Topics**: Dynamic programming on graphs, advanced data structures for speed (e.g., adjacency lists with specialized indexing).

7.4 Additional Resources

- *Introduction to Algorithms* by Cormen, Leiserson, Rivest, and Stein (heavy coverage of graph algorithms).

- Online coding platforms like **LeetCode** or **HackerRank** with specialized graph challenges.

- Libraries (e.g., **NetworkX** in Python) for complex graph modeling and advanced analyses.

By understanding and implementing graph fundamentals, you've taken another major leap in your Data Structures & Algorithms journey. Continue experimenting with different graph structures and algorithms, and let your creativity guide you in applying these powerful tools to real-world problems.

CHAPTER 7: SORTING AND SEARCHING TECHNIQUES

S orting and searching are foundational operations in computer science, integral to countless applications. Efficiently sorting data improves retrieval speed, while fast searching algorithms are essential for quick lookups. This chapter covers:

1. **Overview of Sorting Algorithms**

    o **Bubble Sort, Selection Sort, Insertion Sort, Merge Sort, Quick Sort**

    o Their time complexities, advantages, and drawbacks

2. **Searching Algorithms**

    o **Linear Search vs. Binary Search**

    o Practical use cases and performance considerations

3. **Implementing Sorting and Searching in Python**

    o Step-by-step code for each algorithm

    o Best practices for real-world usage

4. **Analyzing Time and Space Complexity**

    o Big O notation for the sorting and searching techniques

    o Trade-offs among different algorithms

5. **Project: Sorting and Searching User Data Efficiently**

    o Putting it all together to handle realistic scenarios

o   A console-based program to sort user data and perform quick lookups

By the end of this chapter, you'll possess a firm grasp of when and how to apply each sorting and searching algorithm, as well as how to optimize them for performance.

1. Overview of Sorting Algorithms

Sorting organizes data into a meaningful order (e.g., ascending numeric order or alphabetical). Though many sorting algorithms exist, we'll examine five of the most commonly taught:

1.1 Bubble Sort

Concept: Repeatedly compare adjacent elements and swap them if they are out of order. This "bubbles up" the largest or smallest element to its correct position per pass.

Key Points:

- **Worst-Case Time Complexity**: O(n2)O(n^2)O(n2)

- **Best-Case Time Complexity**: O(n)O(n)O(n) (if already sorted and you implement an "early exit" flag)

- **Space Complexity**: O(1)O(1)O(1)

- **Usage**: Rarely used in production due to inefficiency. Great for teaching basic concepts.

Pseudocode:

php

```
bubble_sort(array):

  n = length of array

  for i in 0 to n-1:

    swapped = false
```

```
for j in 0 to n-i-2:

    if array[j] > array[j+1]:

        swap array[j] and array[j+1]

        swapped = true

    if not swapped:

        break  # array is already sorted
```

1.2 Selection Sort

Concept: Select the smallest element in each pass and place it in the correct position at the beginning of the array.

Key Points:

- **Worst-Case and Best-Case Time Complexity**: O(n2)O(n^2)O(n2)

- **Space Complexity**: O(1)O(1)O(1)

- **Usage**: Simple and predictable in terms of comparisons; not very efficient for large datasets.

Pseudocode:

less

```
selection_sort(array):

    n = length of array

    for i in 0 to n-2:

        min_index = i

        for j in i+1 to n-1:

            if array[j] < array[min_index]:

                min_index = j
```

swap array[i] and array[min_index]

1.3 Insertion Sort

Concept: Build a sorted sub-list one element at a time, inserting each new element into its correct position within the sub-list.

Key Points:

- **Worst-Case Time Complexity**: O(n2)O(n^2)O(n2)

- **Best-Case Time Complexity**: O(n)O(n)O(n) (when data is already sorted)

- **Space Complexity**: O(1)O(1)O(1)

- **Usage**: Efficient for very small datasets or nearly sorted data. Also beneficial when data frequently shifts incrementally.

Pseudocode:

c

```
insertion_sort(array):

  for i in 1 to length of array - 1:

    key = array[i]

    j = i - 1

    while j >= 0 and array[j] > key:

      array[j+1] = array[j]

      j -= 1

    array[j+1] = key
```

1.4 Merge Sort

Concept: Divide the array into two halves, recursively sort each half, then merge the two sorted halves.

Key Points:

- **Time Complexity**: $O(n\log n)$ $O(n \log n)$ $O(nlogn)$ in worst and average case

- **Space Complexity**: $O(n)$ $O(n)$ $O(n)$ due to temporary arrays for merging

- **Usage**: Stable sort, ideal for large datasets and parallel sorting. Consistent performance at $O(n\log n)$ $O(n \log n)$ $O(nlogn)$.

Pseudocode:

sql

```
merge_sort(array):

  if length of array > 1:

    mid = length(array) / 2

    left = array[0:mid]

    right = array[mid:end]


    merge_sort(left)

    merge_sort(right)


    # Merge process

    i, j, k = 0, 0, 0

    while i < length(left) and j < length(right):

      if left[i] <= right[j]:

        array[k] = left[i]

        i += 1
```

```
    else:

        array[k] = right[j]

        j += 1

    k += 1


#  any remaining elements

while i < length(left):

    array[k] = left[i]

    i += 1

    k += 1


while j < length(right):

    array[k] = right[j]

    j += 1

    k += 1
```

1.5 Quick Sort

Concept: Select a pivot element and partition the array such that elements less than the pivot go to one side, and those greater than the pivot go to the other side. Recursively sort the sub-arrays.

Key Points:

- **Average Time Complexity**: O(nlog⬚n)O(n \log n)O(nlogn)

- **Worst-Case Time Complexity**: O(n2)O(n^2)O(n2) (if the pivot is consistently the smallest or largest element)

- **Space Complexity**: O(log⬚n)O(\ log n)O(logn) on average for recursion stack

- **Usage**: Often the fastest on average for large datasets if carefully implemented with good pivot selection.

Pseudocode:

sql

```
quick_sort(array, low, high):

  if low < high:

    pivot_index = partition(array, low, high)

    quick_sort(array, low, pivot_index - 1)

    quick_sort(array, pivot_index + 1, high)


partition(array, low, high):

  pivot = array[high]

  i = low - 1

  for j in low to high-1:

    if array[j] <= pivot:

      i += 1

      swap array[i] and array[j]

  swap array[i+1] and array[high]

  return i+1
```

2. Searching Algorithms

2.1 Linear Search

Concept: Iterate through each element until you find the target or reach the end.

Key Points:

- **Time Complexity**: O(n)O(n)O(n)

- **Usage**: Works on unsorted data. Slow if the dataset is large and you need frequent lookups.

Pseudocode:

c

```
linear_search(array, target):

  for i in 0 to length of array - 1:

    if array[i] == target:

      return i

  return -1  # not found
```

2.2 Binary Search

Concept: Compare the target with the middle element. If the target is smaller, search the left half; if larger, search the right half. Repeat until found or sub-array is empty.

Key Points:

- **Time Complexity**: O(log⁡n)O(\log n)O(logn)

- **Precondition**: Data must be sorted

- **Usage**: Quickly finds items in sorted lists or arrays.

Pseudocode:

vbnet

```
binary_search(sorted_array, target):

  low = 0

  high = length(sorted_array) - 1


  while low <= high:

    mid = (low + high) // 2

    if sorted_array[mid] == target:

      return mid

    elif sorted_array[mid] < target:

      low = mid + 1

    else:

      high = mid - 1


  return -1  # not found
```

3. Implementing Sorting and Searching in Python

Below are Python implementations of the described algorithms, along with concise testing functions.

3.1 Bubble Sort in Python

python

```python
def bubble_sort(arr):

    n = len(arr)

    for i in range(n):

        swapped = False

        for j in range(n - i - 1):

            if arr[j] > arr[j + 1]:

                arr[j], arr[j + 1] = arr[j + 1], arr[j]

                swapped = True

        if not swapped:

            break  # List is sorted early

    return arr


def test_bubble_sort():

    print("Testing Bubble Sort:")

    test_arr = [64, 25, 12, 22, 11]

    print("Original:", test_arr)

    sorted_arr = bubble_sort(test_arr[:])

    print("Sorted: ", sorted_arr)
```

3.2 Selection Sort in Python

python

```python
def selection_sort(arr):

    n = len(arr)
```

```python
    for i in range(n):
        min_index = i
        for j in range(i + 1, n):
            if arr[j] < arr[min_index]:
                min_index = j
        arr[i], arr[min_index] = arr[min_index], arr[i]
    return arr


def test_selection_sort():
    print("Testing Selection Sort:")
    test_arr = [64, 25, 12, 22, 11]
    print("Original:", test_arr)
    sorted_arr = selection_sort(test_arr[:])
    print("Sorted: ", sorted_arr)
```

3.3 Insertion Sort in Python

python

```python
def insertion_sort(arr):
    for i in range(1, len(arr)):
        key = arr[i]
        j = i - 1
        while j >= 0 and arr[j] > key:
            arr[j + 1] = arr[j]
```

```python
        j -= 1
    arr[j + 1] = key

    return arr


def test_insertion_sort():
    print("Testing Insertion Sort:")
    test_arr = [64, 25, 12, 22, 11]
    print("Original:", test_arr)
    sorted_arr = insertion_sort(test_arr[:])
    print("Sorted: ", sorted_arr)
```

3.4 Merge Sort in Python

python

```python
def merge_sort(arr):
    if len(arr) > 1:
        mid = len(arr) // 2
        left_half = arr[:mid]
        right_half = arr[mid:]


        merge_sort(left_half)
        merge_sort(right_half)


        i = j = k = 0
```

```python
    while i < len(left_half) and j < len(right_half):

        if left_half[i] <= right_half[j]:

            arr[k] = left_half[i]

            i += 1

        else:

            arr[k] = right_half[j]

            j += 1

        k += 1


    while i < len(left_half):

        arr[k] = left_half[i]

        i += 1

        k += 1


    while j < len(right_half):

        arr[k] = right_half[j]

        j += 1

        k += 1


    return arr


def test_merge_sort():

    print("Testing Merge Sort:")

    test_arr = [64, 25, 12, 22, 11]
```

```python
print("Original:", test_arr)

sorted_arr = merge_sort(test_arr[:])

print("Sorted: ", sorted_arr)
```

3.5 Quick Sort in Python

python

```python
def quick_sort(arr, low, high):
    if low < high:
        pi = partition(arr, low, high)
        quick_sort(arr, low, pi - 1)
        quick_sort(arr, pi + 1, high)
    return arr


def partition(arr, low, high):
    pivot = arr[high]
    i = low - 1
    for j in range(low, high):
        if arr[j] <= pivot:
            i += 1
            arr[i], arr[j] = arr[j], arr[i]
    arr[i + 1], arr[high] = arr[high], arr[i + 1]
    return i + 1
```

```python
def test_quick_sort():

    print("Testing Quick Sort:")

    test_arr = [64, 25, 12, 22, 11]

    print("Original:", test_arr)

    sorted_arr = quick_sort(test_arr[:], 0, len(test_arr) - 1)

    print("Sorted: ", sorted_arr)
```

3.6 Linear Search in Python

python

```python
def linear_search(arr, target):

    for i, val in enumerate(arr):

        if val == target:

            return i

    return -1


def test_linear_search():

    print("Testing Linear Search:")

    test_arr = [10, 20, 30, 40, 50]

    print("Array:", test_arr)

    idx = linear_search(test_arr, 30)

    print("Searching for 30, found index:", idx)

    idx2 = linear_search(test_arr, 99)

    print("Searching for 99, found index:", idx2)
```

3.7 Binary Search in Python

python

```python
def binary_search(arr, target):
    low, high = 0, len(arr) - 1
    while low <= high:
        mid = (low + high) // 2
        if arr[mid] == target:
            return mid
        elif arr[mid] < target:
            low = mid + 1
        else:
            high = mid - 1
    return -1


def test_binary_search():
    print("Testing Binary Search:")
    test_arr = [10, 20, 30, 40, 50]
    print("Array:", test_arr)
    idx = binary_search(test_arr, 30)
    print("Searching for 30, found index:", idx)
    idx2 = binary_search(test_arr, 99)
    print("Searching for 99, found index:", idx2)
```

4. Analyzing Time and Space Complexity

4.1 Sorting Algorithms

Algorithm	Best Case	Average Case	Worst Case	Space	Stability
Bubble Sort	O(n)O(n)O(n)*	O(n2)O(n^2)O(n2)	O(n2)O(n^2)O(n2)	O(1)O(1)O(1)	Stable
Selection Sort	O(n2)O(n^2)O(n2)	O(n2)O(n^2)O(n2)	O(n2)O(n^2)O(n2)	O(1)O(1)O(1)	Not Stable
Insertion Sort	O(n)O(n)O(n)*	O(n2)O(n^2)O(n2)	O(n2)O(n^2)O(n2)	O(1)O(1)O(1)	Stable
Merge Sort	O(nlogn)O(n \log n)O(nlogn)	O(nlogn)O(n \log n)O(nlogn)	O(nlogn)O(n \log n)O(nlogn)	O(n)O(n)O(n)	Stable
Quick Sort	O(nlogn)O(n \log n)O(nlogn)	O(nlogn)O(n \log n)O(nlogn)	O(n2)O(n^2)O(n2)	O(logn)O(\log n)O(logn)	Not always stable

O(n)O(n)O(n) best case for Bubble Sort and Insertion Sort if the array is already sorted (or nearly sorted).

4.2 Searching Algorithms

Algorithm	Time Complexity	Space Complexity	Precondition
Linear Search	O(n)O(n)O(n)	O(1)O(1)O(1)	None (works for unsorted data)
Binary Search	O(logn)O(\log n)O(logn)	O(1)O(1)O(1)	Data must be sorted

5. Project: Sorting and Searching User Data Efficiently

5.1 Project Overview

We'll design a console-based program for managing user data (e.g., IDs or names). The user can:

1. **Add data** to an unsorted list

2. **Choose a sorting algorithm** to sort the data

3. **Perform a search** to quickly find an item

5.2 Data Structure Choice

- **Data**: A list of integers or strings representing user info (IDs, names).

- **Operations**:

  o **Insert**: Append to the list.

  o **Sort**: Apply one of the sorting algorithms (user's choice).

  o **Search**: Use linear or binary search (binary search only if sorted).

5.3 Implementation Outline

python

```python
def display_menu():

    print("\n---- User Data Manager ----")

    print("1. Add Data")

    print("2. View Data")
```

```python
        print("3. Sort Data")

        print("4. Search Data")

        print("5. Exit")


def main():

    data_list = []

    sorted_flag = False


    while True:

        display_menu()

        choice = input("Enter your choice (1-5): ").strip()


        if choice == '1':

            item = input("Enter the data to add (integer or string): ").strip()

            # Try converting to int if possible

            try:

                item = int(item)

            except ValueError:

                pass

            data_list.append(item)

            print(f"'{item}' added to the list.")

            sorted_flag = False


        elif choice == '2':
```

```python
        print("Current Data List:", data_list)


    elif choice == '3':

        print("Select Sorting Algorithm:")

        print(" a) Bubble Sort")

        print(" b) Selection Sort")

        print(" c) Insertion Sort")

        print(" d) Merge Sort")

        print(" e) Quick Sort")

        algo_choice = input("Choose an option (a-e): ").strip()


        if algo_choice == 'a':

            bubble_sort(data_list)

        elif algo_choice == 'b':

            selection_sort(data_list)

        elif algo_choice == 'c':

            insertion_sort(data_list)

        elif algo_choice == 'd':

            merge_sort(data_list)

        elif algo_choice == 'e':

            quick_sort(data_list, 0, len(data_list)-1)

        else:

            print("Invalid choice. No sorting performed.")

            continue
```

```python
        print("Data List after sorting:", data_list)

        sorted_flag = True


elif choice == '4':

    if not data_list:

        print("The list is empty, nothing to search.")

        continue


    target_input = input("Enter the data to search for: ").strip()

    try:

        target_input = int(target_input)

    except ValueError:

        pass


    print("Select Search Algorithm:")

    print(" a) Linear Search")

    print(" b) Binary Search (requires sorted list)")

    search_choice = input("Choose an option (a-b): ").strip()


    if search_choice == 'a':

        index = linear_search(data_list, target_input)

        if index != -1:

            print(f"'{target_input}' found at index {index}.")
```

```python
            else:

                print(f"'{target_input}' not found.")
        elif search_choice == 'b':

            if not sorted_flag:

                print("Data is not sorted. Binary Search may not work correctly.")

            index = binary_search(data_list, target_input)

            if index != -1:

                print(f"'{target_input}' found at index {index}.")

            else:

                print(f"'{target_input}' not found.")
        else:

            print("Invalid choice. No search performed.")


    elif choice == '5':

        print("Exiting User Data Manager. Goodbye!")

        break


    else:

        print("Invalid choice. Please try again.")


if __name__ == "__main__":

    main()
```

5.4 Sample Interaction

sql

---- User Data Manager ----

1. Add Data

2. View Data

3. Sort Data

4. Search Data

5. Exit

Enter your choice (1-5): 1

Enter the data to add (integer or string): 42

'42' added to the list.

---- User Data Manager ----

1. Add Data

2. View Data

3. Sort Data

4. Search Data

5. Exit

Enter your choice (1-5): 1

Enter the data to add (integer or string): 10

'10' added to the list.

---- User Data Manager ----

1. Add Data

2. View Data

3. Sort Data

4. Search Data

5. Exit

Enter your choice (1-5): 2

Current Data List: [42, 10]

---- User Data Manager ----

1. Add Data

2. View Data

3. Sort Data

4. Search Data

5. Exit

Enter your choice (1-5): 3

Select Sorting Algorithm:

 a) Bubble Sort

 b) Selection Sort

 c) Insertion Sort

 d) Merge Sort

 e) Quick Sort

Choose an option (a-e): d

Data List after sorting: [10, 42]

---- User Data Manager ----

1. Add Data

2. View Data

3. Sort Data

4. Search Data

5. Exit

Enter your choice (1-5): 4

Enter the data to search for: 42

Select Search Algorithm:

a) Linear Search

b) Binary Search (requires sorted list)

Choose an option (a-b): b

'42' found at index 1.

---- User Data Manager ----

...

Enter your choice (1-5): 5

Exiting User Data Manager. Goodbye!

6. Conclusion & Next Steps

6.1 Key Takeaways

1. **Sorting Algorithms**

   o **Bubble, Selection, Insertion**: Simple to implement, but typically $O(n2)O(n^2)O(n2)$ in average/worst cases.

- o **Merge, Quick**: More efficient $O(nlogn)O(n \log n)O(nlogn)$ on average. Merge Sort is stable, Quick Sort often faster in practice but can degrade to $O(n2)O(n^2)O(n2)$ in the worst case.

2. **Searching Algorithms**

   - o **Linear Search**: Works on unsorted data but is $O(n)O(n)O(n)$.

   - o **Binary Search**: $O(logn)O(\log n)O(logn)$ but requires sorted data.

3. **Time & Space Complexity**

   - o **Understanding Big O** helps you choose the right algorithm for your data size and constraints.

   - o In real-world scenarios, stable sorts, small overhead, and average-case performance often matter more than worst-case theory.

4. **Project**

   - o Demonstrated how to integrate sorting and searching into a practical application.

   - o Showcased the importance of consistent data states (e.g., "sorted" flag) for correct search.

6.2 Reflections

Sorting and searching are bedrocks of Data Structures & Algorithms. Mastery of these techniques paves the way for handling more specialized data transformations and retrieval operations. While modern languages often provide built-in, optimized methods (like Python's sort() and bisect or C++'s std::sort), understanding the mechanics enables you to troubleshoot performance bottlenecks and adapt these algorithms to custom scenarios.

6.3 Next Steps

1. **Advanced Sorting**: Investigate **Heap Sort**, **Counting Sort**, **Radix Sort**, and **TimSort** (used by Python's built-in sort).

2. **Search Enhancements**: Explore **interpolation search** for numeric data and **ternary search** for unimodal functions.

3.   **Practical Variations**:

   o   **Multi-key sorting**: Sorting by multiple criteria (e.g., last name, then first name).

   o   **In-place vs. out-of-place**: Minimizing additional memory usage.

Additional Resources:

- *Algorithms (4th Edition)* by Robert Sedgewick and Kevin Wayne.

- Online platforms like **LeetCode, HackerRank, GeeksforGeeks** for practice.

With these foundational sorting and searching skills, you're poised to tackle more complex data manipulation tasks. Use the knowledge gained here as a launchpad for optimizing performance in all sorts of applications, from data analytics to real-time systems.

CHAPTER 8: **RECURSION AND DYNAMIC PROGRAMMING**

ecursion and Dynamic Programming (DP) are pivotal problem-solving techniques in computer science, enabling you to handle complex tasks by breaking them into manageable subproblems. Recursion solves problems by having functions call themselves, while Dynamic Programming optimizes recursive solutions by storing intermediate results, thus avoiding repeated calculations. In this chapter, we delve into the fundamental concepts of recursion, explore memoization and tabulation (the two primary DP techniques), and demonstrate how to implement dynamic programming solutions in Python. We culminate with a hands-on project solving the **Knapsack Problem** for resource allocation, illustrating the power and elegance of DP in real-world scenarios.

1. Understanding Recursion

1.1 The Recursive Paradigm

Recursion occurs when a function calls itself in order to solve a problem. This self-referential technique relies on:

1. **Base Case**: A condition under which the function returns a straightforward answer without further recursive calls.

2. **Recursive Case**: The scenario in which the function calls itself with a subset or simpler form of the original problem.

Why Use Recursion?

- **Clarity**: Some problems (like traversing tree structures) map naturally to recursive solutions.

- **Divide and Conquer**: You can split a large problem into smaller subproblems that share the same structure, making your code simpler to reason about.

- **Mathematical Elegance**: Many mathematical concepts (factorials, Fibonacci numbers, etc.) have direct recursive definitions.

1.2 Anatomy of a Recursive Function

Take the classic **factorial** example (n!n!n!):

$n!=\{1$ if $n \le 1n \times (n-1)!$ if $n>1n! = \begin{cases} 1 & \text{if } n \le 1 \\ n \times (n-1)! & \text{if } n > 1 \end{cases}n!=\{1n \times (n-1)!$ if $n \le 1$ if $n>1$

In Python, it translates to:

- python

-

- def factorial(n):

-   if n <= 1:   # Base Case

-     return 1

-   else:

-     return n * factorial(n - 1) # Recursive Case

Key Considerations:

- **Infinite Recursion**: Occurs if you omit or incorrectly define the base case.

- **Stack Depth**: Each recursive call adds to the call stack. Deep recursions might trigger a stack overflow if you exceed Python's recursion limit.

- **Efficiency**: Naive recursion can repeat identical subcomputations, leading to exponential time complexity—this is where **Dynamic Programming** often steps in.

1.3 Common Recursive Patterns

1. **Tail Recursion** (less relevant in Python due to lack of tail-call optimization).

2. **Divide and Conquer**: Split the problem (e.g., merge sort, quick sort).

3. **Backtracking**: Systematically explore possibilities (e.g., DFS in graphs, Sudoku solvers).

4. **Tree/Graph Traversals**: Move down children or neighbors.

Recursion forms a natural foundation for many DP solutions, as you typically write a naive recursive formula, then optimize it.

2. Memoization and Tabulation Techniques

Dynamic Programming is the strategy of **breaking down** complex problems into subproblems and **storing** (or "remembering") their results to avoid redundant computations. There are two main approaches:

2.1 Memoization

Memoization is a **top-down** approach. You start with the original (often recursive) function, and each time you compute a subproblem's result, you cache it in a dictionary or array. On subsequent requests for that subproblem, you return the cached result instead of recalculating.

Conceptual Steps:

1. Write a normal recursive function that solves the problem.

2. Add a data structure (hash map/dictionary in Python) to store results of subproblems.

3. Before computing a subproblem, check if it's in the cache. If yes, return it immediately. Otherwise, compute it, store it in the cache, then return it.

Example: Fibonacci with Memoization

Naive Fibonacci recursion:

$$F(n) = \begin{cases} n, & n < 2 \\ F(n-1) + F(n-2), & n \ge 2 \end{cases}$$

This is exponential in time without memoization, since many calls overlap. With memoization:

- python
-
- def fib_memo(n, cache=None):
- if cache is None:
- cache = {}
- if n < 2:
- return n
-
- if n in cache:
- return cache[n]
-
- cache[n] = fib_memo(n-1, cache) + fib_memo(n-2, cache)
- return cache[n]

Benefits:

- Straightforward if you already have a recursive solution.
- Minimal modifications required to add caching logic.

Drawbacks:

- May consume memory if subproblem space is large.

- Recursive depth remains a limiting factor.

2.2 Tabulation

Tabulation is a **bottom-up** approach. Instead of starting from the original function call, you systematically solve all smaller subproblems first, storing their answers in a table (array), and build up until you reach the final solution.

Conceptual Steps:

1. Identify the subproblems and an ordering in which they must be solved.

2. Create a table (array or 2D array) to store the results of each subproblem.

3. Fill the table iteratively, using previously computed values to get the new ones.

Example: Fibonacci with Tabulation

- python

-

- def fib_tab(n):

- if n < 2:

- return n

-

- table = [0] * (n+1)

- table[0] = 0

- table[1] = 1

- for i in range(2, n+1):

- table[i] = table[i-1] + table[i-2]

- return table[n]

Benefits:

- No recursion overhead — avoids deep call stacks.

- Often yields a straightforward iteration pattern.

Drawbacks:

- You must carefully figure out the correct order of filling the table.

- Potential for large memory usage if the subproblem space is big.

2.3 Choosing Memoization vs. Tabulation

- **Memoization**: Great if you already have a recursive solution or if the subproblem space might not require filling every cell (sparse usage).

- **Tabulation**: Often slightly more efficient in constant factors, avoids recursion depth issues, and ensures each subproblem is solved exactly once in a clear order.

In many cases, either approach is valid, and performance differences may be minor for typical input sizes.

3. Implementing Dynamic Programming Solutions in Python

3.1 Example 1: Factorial with Memoization

Although factorial can be computed directly, it illustrates how memoization typically works:

- python

```
def factorial_memo(n, cache=None):

    if cache is None:

        cache = {}

    if n <= 1:

        return 1

    if n in cache:

        return cache[n]

    result = n * factorial_memo(n-1, cache)

    cache[n] = result

    return result
```

3.2 Example 2: Factorial with Tabulation

```
python


def factorial_tab(n):

    if n <= 1:

        return 1

    table = [0]*(n+1)

    table[0] = 1

    table[1] = 1

    for i in range(2, n+1):
```

- table[i] = i * table[i-1]

- return table[n]

3.3 Example 3: Fibonacci (Memo vs. Tab)

We've already seen code for both **fib_memo** and **fib_tab**. Let's illustrate typical run times:

- python

-

- import time

-

- def test_fib(n=35):

-     start = time.time()

-     print("fib_memo:", fib_memo(n))

-     mid = time.time()

-     print("Memo time:", mid - start)

-

-     print("fib_tab:", fib_tab(n))

-     end = time.time()

-     print("Tab time:", end - mid)

-

- if __name__ == "__main__":

-     test_fib()

You'd expect both DP approaches to run in roughly O(n)O(n)O(n) for Fibonacci, as opposed to O(2n)O(2^n)O(2n) for the naive recursive method.

3.4 Example 4: Edit Distance

Another famous DP problem is the **Edit Distance (Levenshtein Distance)** between two strings, measuring how many operations (insert, delete, substitute) are needed to transform one string into another. While we won't delve deeply here, its tabulation approach is a classic:

- python
-
- def edit_distance(s1, s2):
-     m, n = len(s1), len(s2)
-     dp = [[0]*(n+1) for _ in range(m+1)]
-
-     # Base cases
-     for i in range(m+1):
-         dp[i][0] = i
-     for j in range(n+1):
-         dp[0][j] = j
-
-     # Fill the table
-     for i in range(1, m+1):
-         for j in range(1, n+1):
-             if s1[i-1] == s2[j-1]:
-                 dp[i][j] = dp[i-1][j-1]
-             else:

- dp[i][j] = 1 + min(

- dp[i-1][j],   # deletion

- dp[i][j-1],   # insertion

- dp[i-1][j-1] # substitution

-)

- return dp[m][n]

Key DP Takeaways:

1. Identify **overlapping subproblems**.

2. Detect an optimal substructure: The solution to the larger problem can be built from solutions to subproblems.

3. Decide between **memoization** (top-down) and **tabulation** (bottom-up).

4. Project: Solving the Knapsack Problem for Resource Allocation

4.1 Knapsack Problem Overview

The **0/1 Knapsack Problem** is a classic in computer science, describing:

- A knapsack (or bag) with a **capacity** (maximum weight it can hold).

- A set of **items**, each with a **weight** and **value** (or profit).

- The goal is to **maximize the total value** of items you can put into the bag **without exceeding** the capacity.

Formally, let:

- nnn be the number of items.

- WWW be the capacity of the knapsack.

- w_i be the weight of item i.

- v_i be the value of item i.

The 0/1 knapsack constraint means each item can either be taken **whole** or **not at all** (no partial fractions).

4.2 Recursive Formulation

We can define a recursive solution:

$$\text{knapsack}(i, C) = \begin{cases} 0, & \text{if } i < 0 \text{ or } C \le 0 \\ \max(\text{knapsack}(i-1, C), \quad v_i + \text{knapsack}(i-1, C - w_i)), & \text{if } w_i \le C \\ \text{knapsack}(i-1, C), & \text{if } w_i > C \end{cases}$$

- **Base Case**: If $i < 0$ or capacity $C \le 0$, the value is zero.

- **Recursive Case**:

    1. **Exclude** the current item (i) → $\text{knapsack}(i-1, C)$.

    2. **Include** the current item if $w_i \le C$ → $v_i + \text{knapsack}(i-1, C - w_i)$.

The maximum of those two paths is your optimal value.

4.3 Implementing with Memoization

- python

-

- def knapsack_memo(weights, values, capacity, n, cache=None):

- # n is the index of current item (last item in 0-based index)

- # capacity is remaining capacity in the knapsack

-

- if cache is None:

- cache = {}

-

- # Base conditions

- if capacity <= 0 or n < 0:

- return 0

-

- # Check cache

- if (n, capacity) in cache:

- return cache[(n, capacity)]

-

- # If item cannot be included due to weight constraints

- if weights[n] > capacity:

- result = knapsack_memo(weights, values, capacity, n-1, cache)

- else:

- # Two choices: exclude or include

- exclude_val = knapsack_memo(weights, values, capacity, n-1, cache)

- include_val = values[n] + knapsack_memo(weights, values, capacity - weights[n], n-1, cache)

- result = max(exclude_val, include_val)

-

- cache[(n, capacity)] = result

- return result

4.4 Implementing with Tabulation

We can create a 2D table dpdpdp of size $(n+1)\times(capacity+1)(n+1) \times (capacity+1)(n+1)\times(capacity+1)$, where dp[i][c]dp[i][c]dp[i][c] represents the maximum value achievable using items from 000 to iii with capacity ccc.

Steps:

1. Initialize dpdpdp with zeros.

2. Iterate through items iii from 0 to n-1.

3. For each capacity ccc from 0 to WWW:

   ○ If $wi \le cw\_i \le cwi \le c$: dp[i+1][c]=max⬚(dp[i][c], vi+dp[i][c−wi])dp[i+1][c] = \max(dp[i][c], \; v_i + dp[i][c - w_i])dp[i+1][c]=max(dp[i][c],vi+dp[i][c−wi])

   ○ Else: dp[i+1][c]=dp[i][c]dp[i+1][c] = dp[i][c]dp[i+1][c]=dp[i][c]

Code:

- python

-

- def knapsack_tab(weights, values, capacity):

- n = len(weights)

- # dp array with dimensions (n+1) x (capacity+1)

- dp = [[0]*(capacity+1) for _ in range(n+1)]

-

- for i in range(1, n+1):

- w = weights[i-1]

- v = values[i-1]

- for c in range(1, capacity+1):

- if w <= c:

- dp[i][c] = max(dp[i-1][c], v + dp[i-1][c - w])

- else:

- dp[i][c] = dp[i-1][c]

-

- return dp[n][capacity]

4.5 Building a Console-Based Resource Allocation Program

4.5.1 Project Specifications

- **Input**: List of "items" (could be tasks, resources) with a weight (cost or usage) and a value (benefit). A maximum capacity (budget or limit).

- **Output**: The maximum total value possible without exceeding the capacity.

- **Implementation**: Provide both memoized and tabulated solutions, letting the user compare.

4.5.2 Sample Code

- python

-

- def display_knapsack_menu():

- print("\n--- Knapsack Resource Allocation ---")

- print("1. Add an item (weight, value)")

- print("2. View items")

```python
    print("3. Set capacity")

    print("4. Solve Knapsack (Memoization)")

    print("5. Solve Knapsack (Tabulation)")

    print("6. Exit")


def knapsack_main():
    items = []
    capacity = 0

    while True:
        display_knapsack_menu()
        choice = input("Enter your choice (1-6): ").strip()

        if choice == '1':
            w = int(input("Enter weight: "))
            v = int(input("Enter value: "))
            items.append((w, v))
            print(f"Added item with weight={w}, value={v}.")

        elif choice == '2':
            print("Current items:")
            for i, (w, v) in enumerate(items):
```

```python
    print(f"Item {i}: weight={w}, value={v}")


elif choice == '3':

    capacity = int(input("Enter knapsack capacity: "))

    print(f"Capacity set to {capacity}.")


elif choice == '4':

    if not items or capacity <= 0:

        print("No items or invalid capacity.")

        continue

    weights = [x[0] for x in items]

    values = [x[1] for x in items]

    n = len(items) - 1

    result = knapsack_memo(weights, values, capacity, n)

    print(f"Maximum value (memo) with capacity={capacity}: {result}")


elif choice == '5':

    if not items or capacity <= 0:

        print("No items or invalid capacity.")

        continue

    weights = [x[0] for x in items]

    values = [x[1] for x in items]
```

```python
        result = knapsack_tab(weights, values, capacity)

        print(f"Maximum value (tab) with capacity={capacity}: {result}")


    elif choice == '6':

        print("Exiting Knapsack Resource Allocation.")

        break


    else:

        print("Invalid choice. Please try again.")


if __name__ == "__main__":

    knapsack_main()
```

4.5.3 Sample Interaction

```sql

--- Knapsack Resource Allocation ---

1. Add an item (weight, value)

2. View items

3. Set capacity

4. Solve Knapsack (Memoization)

5. Solve Knapsack (Tabulation)

6. Exit
```

- Enter your choice (1-6): 1

- Enter weight: 2

- Enter value: 4

- Added item with weight=2, value=4.

-

- --- Knapsack Resource Allocation ---

- ...

- Enter your choice (1-6): 1

- Enter weight: 3

- Enter value: 5

- Added item with weight=3, value=5.

-

- --- Knapsack Resource Allocation ---

- ...

- Enter your choice (1-6): 2

- Current items:

- Item 0: weight=2, value=4

- Item 1: weight=3, value=5

-

- --- Knapsack Resource Allocation ---

- ...

- Enter your choice (1-6): 3

- Enter knapsack capacity: 3

- Capacity set to 3.

-

- --- Knapsack Resource Allocation ---

- ...

- Enter your choice (1-6): 4

- Maximum value (memo) with capacity=3: 5

-

- --- Knapsack Resource Allocation ---

- ...

- Enter your choice (1-6): 5

- Maximum value (tab) with capacity=3: 5

-

- --- Knapsack Resource Allocation ---

- ...

- Enter your choice (1-6): 6

- Exiting Knapsack Resource Allocation.

Here, with capacity=3, you can't pick both items (2 + 3 = 5 > 3), so the best pick is the item with weight=3, value=5, giving a total value of 5.

5. Troubleshooting and Problem-Solving

5.1 Common Pitfalls

1. **Missing Base Cases**: For recursion, forgetting base cases leads to infinite recursion.

2. **Incorrect Table Dimensions**: For tabulation, the 2D array size might be off by 1 or incorrectly indexed.

3. **Overlapping Subproblems Not Identified**: Some problems appear recursive but lack repeated subproblems, making DP less beneficial.

4. **Memory Overuse**: Large DP tables may exceed available memory if the state space is huge.

5. **Time Complexity Surprises**: DP solutions are typically polynomial, but for some problems (like multi-dimensional knapsack), the polynomial might still be large.

5.2 Debugging Tips

1. **Print Intermediate States**: For memoization, print the cache content. For tabulation, display partial rows.

2. **Use Small Examples**: Validate correctness with minimal test cases, manually verifying each step.

3. **Compare Recursive, Memoized, and Tabulated Outputs**: They should match, ensuring consistency.

4. **Check Edge Cases**: Zero capacity, zero items, extremely large capacity relative to item weights, etc.

5.3 Performance Considerations

- **Memoization**: Potentially uses less memory if many states remain unvisited. But deep recursion might cause overhead or stack limits.

- **Tabulation**: Often faster in practice due to iterative approach, but can't skip states if table-filling is over a large range.

- **Optimizations**:

  o **Space Optimization**: Sometimes you can compress 2D DP to 1D if your transitions only rely on the previous row.

  o **Iterative vs. Recursive**: In Python, iterative solutions avoid recursion-depth limits.

6. Conclusion & Next Steps

6.1 Key Takeaways

1. **Recursion**

   o Functions call themselves, simplifying complex, self-similar problems.

   o Essential to define clear base cases and understand stack usage.

2. **Dynamic Programming**

   o **Memoization** (top-down) and **Tabulation** (bottom-up) mitigate redundant subcomputations.

   o Effective where overlapping subproblems and an optimal substructure exist.

3. **Knapsack Problem**

   o Demonstrates how DP elegantly solves combinatorial optimization tasks.

   o Showcases the difference between naive recursion (exponential) vs. DP (polynomial).

6.2 Reflections

Recursion alone can be exponential if the same subproblem recurs multiple times. **Dynamic Programming** addresses this by storing solutions to these subproblems. Mastery of DP equips you to handle a wide range of algorithmic challenges—route planning, scheduling, string operations (like edit distance), and more.

6.3 Future Directions

1. **Advanced Knapsack Variants**:

    o   **Unbounded Knapsack** (unlimited items).

    o   **Knapsack with multiple constraints** (multiple resource limits).

2. **Complex DP Problems**:

    o   **Longest Increasing Subsequence**

    o   **Shortest Path in Graphs** (Bellman-Ford, Floyd-Warshall)

    o   **Game Theory** (minimax with DP)

3. **Optimized Strategies**:

    o   1D space optimization for Knapsack.

    o   More advanced data structures for large or streaming data.

Additional Resources:

-   *Introduction to Algorithms* by Cormen, Leiserson, Rivest, and Stein (deep coverage of DP).

-   Online judges (LeetCode, HackerRank, Codeforces) to practice a variety of DP problems.

With recursion and DP in your toolkit, you're equipped to tackle advanced algorithmic challenges, systematically handling large problem spaces. Embrace the incremental approach—identify subproblems, decide on memoization or tabulation, and implement solutions that scale efficiently.

CHAPTER 9: ADVANCED TOPICS AND ALGORITHM OPTIMIZATION

T his chapter delves into several advanced data structures—**Heaps**, **Priority Queues**, **Tries**, and **Suffix Trees**—and provides a deeper look into **Algorithm Efficiency** using **Big O Notation**. We'll discuss **Code Optimization** strategies for better performance and walk through a project on identifying and improving bottlenecks in existing applications.

1. Heaps and Priority Queues

1.1 Understanding Heaps

A **heap** is a specialized tree-based data structure that satisfies the **heap property**:

- **Max-Heap**: The value of each node is **greater** than or equal to the values of its children.

- **Min-Heap**: The value of each node is **less** than or equal to the values of its children.

Heaps are often implemented as **binary trees**, stored in arrays for efficiency:

1. **Indexing**:

   o   Root node at index 0.

   o   For node at index iii, its children are at **2*i + 1** (left) and **2*i + 2** (right).

2. **Applications**:

   o **Priority Queues**: In a **min-heap**, the smallest element is at the root, ensuring removal of the minimum or maximum is always $O(\log n)$.

   o **Heapsort**: A sorting algorithm that leverages the heap structure to achieve $O(n \log n)$ time.

   o **Graph Algorithms**: Dijkstra's shortest path often uses a min-priority queue for selecting the next closest node.

1.2 Priority Queues

A **priority queue** is an abstract data type where each element has a "priority." The element with the highest (or lowest) priority is served before others. **Heaps** typically back priority queues, as removing or inserting an element of highest priority can happen efficiently in $O(\log n)$.

Common Operations:

1. **Insert** or **push** an element with a given priority.

2. **Pop** the highest/lowest priority element (depending on min or max orientation).

3. **Peek** at the root to see the current minimum or maximum.

Example in Python using heapq for a min-heap:

python

```
import heapq


def min_heap_example():
  heap = []
  # Push elements (value only, acts as priority)
  heapq.heappush(heap, 5)
```

```
heapq.heappush(heap, 1)

heapq.heappush(heap, 3)


print("Min element:", heap[0])  # 1

smallest = heapq.heappop(heap)  # Removes and returns smallest

print("Popped:", smallest)     # 1

print("Heap now:", heap)       # [3, 5]
```

For **max-heap** behavior, you can store negative values (priority * -1) or use a custom comparator.

2. Tries and Suffix Trees

2.1 Tries (Prefix Trees)

A **trie** is a tree-like data structure for storing strings by their **prefixes**. Each node typically represents a character in the path from the root. By traversing the trie, you can check common prefixes rapidly.

Key Operations:

1. **Insert a word**: Traverse each character; if the node doesn't exist, create it, then mark the end of the word.

2. **Search for a word**: Follow the path for each character; if any node is missing, the word isn't present.

3. **Prefix Queries**: Quickly find all words starting with a given prefix.

Example: Suppose you insert ["cat", "car", "cap"]:

arduino

```
(root)
└── 'c'
    └── 'a'
        ├── 't' (end-of-word: "cat")
        ├── 'r' (end-of-word: "car")
        └── 'p' (end-of-word: "cap")
```

Implementation Skeleton:

python

```python
class TrieNode:
    def __init__(self):
        self.children = {}
        self.is_end_of_word = False


class Trie:
    def __init__(self):
        self.root = TrieNode()


    def insert(self, word):
        current = self.root
        for char in word:
            if char not in current.children:
                current.children[char] = TrieNode()
            current = current.children[char]
```

```
current.is_end_of_word = True


def search(self, word):

    current = self.root

    for char in word:

        if char not in current.children:

            return False

        current = current.children[char]

    return current.is_end_of_word
```

Applications:

- **Autocomplete** systems.

- **Spell-checkers**.

- **Routing tables** in networking.

2.2 Suffix Trees

A **suffix tree** is a compressed trie of **all suffixes** of a given string.

- For a string SSS of length nnn, it has nnn suffixes.

- A suffix tree can answer substring queries in $O(m)O(m)O(m)$ time, where mmm is the query length.

- Construction can be done in $O(n)O(n)O(n)$ (e.g., Ukkonen's algorithm), though the details are quite complex.

Suffix Tree vs. Suffix Array:

- **Suffix Array**: A sorted array of all suffixes; uses less memory, simpler to implement.

- **Suffix Tree**: More powerful for certain advanced queries (longest repeated substring, etc.).

- **Suffix Automaton**: Another related structure with memory and complexity advantages.

Common Use Cases:

- **Text indexing**: Quickly check if a substring exists.

- **Longest repeated substring** problems.

- **Bioinformatics**: Searching genetic sequences.

3. Analyzing Algorithm Efficiency with Big O Notation

3.1 Big O Basics

Big O Notation describes how an algorithm's runtime or space requirement grows with the input size nnn. While prior chapters introduced the concept, we now dig deeper into:

1. **Asymptotic Behavior**: Focuses on large nnn.

2. **Dominant Terms**: Lower-order terms and constants are ignored (e.g., $O(5n+3) \equiv O(n) O(5n + 3) \equiv O(n) O(5n+3) \equiv O(n)$).

3. **Upper Bound**: Big O is an upper bound on growth rate; other notations (Big Omega, Theta) refine lower/average bounds.

3.2 Common Big O Classes

1. **O(1)**: Constant time. Access by index in an array is typically $O(1) O(1) O(1)$.

2. **O(\log n)**: Logarithmic. Binary search in a sorted array.

3. **O(n)**: Linear. Scanning a list.

4. **O(n \log n)**: Common in divide-and-conquer sorts (Merge Sort, Quick Sort average).

5. **O(n^2):** Nested loops in naive approaches.

6. **O(2^n), O(n!):** Exponential, factorial growth often found in brute force solutions for complex combinatorial problems.

3.3 Amortized Analysis

- **Amortized Cost**: Averages the cost of operations over a sequence, especially in data structures like **dynamic arrays** or **hash tables** where occasional expensive operations are offset by many cheap ones.

- Example: Appending to a dynamic array is $O(1)O(1)O(1)$ amortized, though resizing can cost $O(n)O(n)O(n)$ at specific moments.

3.4 Practical Performance Considerations

1. **Constant Factors**: Even if two solutions share the same Big O class, differences in constants or cache locality might matter.

2. **Data Sizes**: For small nnn, a simpler $O(n2)O(n^2)O(n2)$ might outperform a complex $O(nlog⁡n)O(n \log n)O(nlogn)$ solution with a large constant overhead.

3. **Hardware Dependencies**: CPU cache, memory bandwidth, and parallel execution can affect real-world results.

4. Optimizing Code for Performance

4.1 Identifying Bottlenecks

1. **Profiling**: Use Python's built-in cProfile or timeit to measure where time is spent.

2. **Memory Usage**: Tools like memory_profiler or inspection of data structure sizes to detect excessive memory consumption.

3. **Hot Spots**: Look for loops in your code that run too many times, or nested recursion that duplicates work.

4.2 Common Optimization Strategies

1. **Algorithmic**: Move from $O(n2)O(n\text{^2})O(n2)$ to $O(n\log n)O(n \log n)O(n\log n)$. This is typically the biggest win.

2. **Data Structures**: Use a more suitable structure—deque instead of list for queue operations, or a **HashMap** instead of a list search.

3. **Caching/Memoization**: If repeated computations occur, store results.

4. **Batch Operations**: Minimize overhead by grouping tasks (e.g., vectorized operations in NumPy).

5. **Parallelization**: In CPU-bound tasks, consider concurrent or parallel approaches (though Python's GIL can limit pure threading efficiency).

6. **I/O Bound Optimization**: For large file operations or network requests, reduce or pipeline I/O where possible.

4.3 Python-Specific Tips

1. **Built-in Functions**: Python's built-ins (e.g., sum, sorted) are optimized in C.

2. **List Comprehensions**: Often faster than manual for loops.

3. **Use collections.deque** for efficient queue ops.

4. **Avoid Unnecessary Conversions** or ing of data structures.

5. **Vectorized Libraries**: If numeric computations dominate, rely on **NumPy** or **pandas** for performance.

5. Project: Enhancing the Performance of Existing Applications

5.1 Project Overview

We'll take an existing application—perhaps a naive search or sorting routine—and profile it, then replace the slow algorithmic portions with more optimal data structures or approaches. This demonstrates a real-world scenario of incremental optimization.

Hypothetical Scenario

- **Application**: A user manager that maintains a list of users and frequently searches for usernames.

- **Current Approach**: Linear searching a Python list for each query (inefficient for large user bases).

- **Goal**: Improve search times using advanced structures (binary search if sorted, or a HashMap, or a Trie for prefix-based lookups).

5.2 Step 1: Profiling the Current Code

python

```python
import time

import random

import string


def generate_users(n):

    # random strings

    users = []
```

```python
    for _ in range(n):

        user = ''.join(random.choices(string.ascii_lowercase, k=7))

        users.append(user)

    return users


def naive_search(users, target):

    for user in users:

        if user == target:

            return True

    return False


def main_naive():

    user_list = generate_users(100000)  # 100k users

    target = user_list[50000]


    start = time.time()

    found = naive_search(user_list, target)

    end = time.time()


    print("Found?", found, "Time:", end - start)


if __name__ == "__main__":

    main_naive()
```

Run **main_naive** and observe run time. Suppose it takes 0.2 seconds for each search (example measurement).

5.3 Step 2: Introduce Data Structure Optimization

Approach A: Convert user_list into a **set** (hash-based), so membership checks are $O(1)O(1)O(1)$ on average.

python

```python
def optimized_search(users_set, target):
    return target in users_set  # O(1) average
```

Implementation:

python

```python
def main_optimized():
    user_list = generate_users(100000)
    users_set = set(user_list)  # O(n) to build set once
    target = user_list[50000]

    import time
    start = time.time()
    found = (target in users_set)
    end = time.time()

    print("Found?", found, "Time:", end - start)
```

We expect a significant speedup: searching 100k items with a set membership check is typically very fast, often microseconds rather than milliseconds.

5.4 Step 3: Further Optimization or Additional Features

- **Use a Trie** if you need prefix-based queries (e.g., autocomplete partial usernames).

- **Use Sorting + Binary Search** if you frequently do range queries (like everything between "alice" and "bob").

- **Maintain a Balanced Tree** or **B-Tree** (less common in pure Python, but conceptually relevant for large data in DB systems).

5.5 Step 4: Compare and Validate Improvements

1. **Time**: Record time for searching random targets.

2. **Memory**: sys.getsizeof(users_set) vs. sys.getsizeof(user_list) or monitor usage with memory_profiler.

Wrap-Up:

- **Check** correctness: We must preserve the functional behavior (ensuring the user is found or not).

- **Document** changes, so future maintainers understand why a set or trie is used.

5.6 Additional Real-World Considerations

- **Synchronization**: If multiple threads update the data structure, concurrency control or thread-safe structures might be needed.

- **Persistence**: For large data, you might store data structures on disk (DB systems, noSQL with indexing).

- **Scaling**: If user data hits millions, you might consider partitioning or sharding across servers.

6. Conclusion & Next Steps

6.1 Key Takeaways

1. **Heaps and Priority Queues**

   o   Min/Max Heaps enable efficient top-priority element retrieval.

   o   Useful in scheduling tasks, implementing Dijkstra's, or building heap-based sorts.

2. **Tries and Suffix Trees**

   o   Ideal for prefix-based searches (Tries) or substring queries (Suffix Trees).

   o   Support fast insertions and lookups for string-centric applications.

3. **Algorithm Efficiency**

   o   Big O notation frames how runtime grows with input size.

   o   Amortized analysis clarifies average costs across multiple operations.

4. **Optimizing Existing Code**

   o   Profile to find hotspots.

   o   Choose improved algorithms or data structures for major performance gains.

   o   Validate correctness and keep in mind real-world constraints like memory usage.

6.2 Next Steps

- **Explore Additional Data Structures**:

- o **Segment Trees, Fenwick Trees (Binary Indexed Trees)** for range queries.

- o **Disjoint Set/Union-Find** for connectivity queries.

- **Advanced Optimization Techniques**:

    - o **Parallel/Concurrent Programming** in Python (multiprocessing, async I/O).

    - o **JIT Compilation** (e.g., PyPy or Numba for numeric code).

- **Further Real-World Projects**:

    - o Building a **Priority Task Scheduler** using a min-heap.

    - o Implementing a **String Search Engine** with tries/suffix arrays for partial matches.

Resources:

- *Algorithms* by Robert Sedgewick, Kevin Wayne (heaps, tries).

- *Introduction to Algorithms* by Cormen et al. (suffix trees, advanced data structures).

- Python libraries (heapq, bisect, collections) for built-in optimizations.

6.3 Final Thoughts

By leveraging advanced structures like heaps and tries, refining your understanding of Big O, and systematically optimizing code, you can handle complex data-centric challenges efficiently. Remember that real-world performance hinges on the right balance of **algorithmic complexity**, **data structure choice**, and **practical profiling**. Continue exploring additional specialized structures and keep measuring performance to ensure your solutions remain robust and optimized.

CHAPTER 10: REAL-WORLD APPLICATIONS, PROJECTS, AND INTERVIEW PREPARATION

Having explored core data structures, algorithms, and advanced optimizations, this final chapter shifts the focus to how these concepts **apply to real-world industries** like healthcare, finance, and technology. We will examine **case studies** of successful DS&A implementations, undertake a **comprehensive project** that integrates multiple data structures and algorithms, and discuss **practical strategies** for **technical interviews**. We'll also address common **troubleshooting** and **debugging** techniques, and provide **next steps** to continue your DS&A learning journey.

1. Data Structures and Algorithms in Healthcare, Finance, and Technology

1.1 Healthcare Applications

1. **Patient Data Management**

    o **Data Structures**: Linked lists or trees for managing patient records; hash tables for quick lookups by patient ID.

    o **Algorithms**: Encryption or secure hashing to protect sensitive data, BFS or DFS for healthcare network analysis (e.g., disease contact tracing).

2. **Medical Imaging and Diagnostics**

- o **Graph Algorithms**: Region-growing or segmentation in MRI/CT scans, often employing BFS/DFS to detect connected components.

- o **Dynamic Programming**: Pattern recognition or detection of anomalies in images.

3. **Scheduling and Resource Allocation**

- o **Heaps (Priority Queues)**: Managing priority-based patient scheduling.

- o **Knapsack Problem Variants**: Allocating limited hospital resources (beds, ICU units) to maximize patient outcomes.

1.2 Finance Applications

1. **Stock Market Analysis**

- o **Priority Queues** for order matching in real-time trading systems.

- o **Graph or Tree Structures** for hierarchical company data (fund of funds, etc.).

2. **Risk Assessment and Credit Scoring**

- o **Decision Trees** or tries for classification.

- o **DP or Greedy** algorithms to optimize portfolio distributions.

3. **Blockchain and Distributed Ledgers**

- o **Merkle Trees** for fast verification of transactions.

- o **Hash Tables** for quick lookups of blocks/transactions.

1.3 Technology & E-Commerce

1. **Search and Recommendation Systems**

- o **Tries** for autocomplete, suffix arrays/trees for text queries.

- o **Graph Algorithms** (PageRank-like approaches) in social media or product recommendation.

2. Load Balancing and Cloud Infrastructure

- o **Heaps** (priority scheduling) for tasks or containers.

- o **Graphs** to model network topologies, BFS/DFS or shortest paths for routing.

3. Big Data Analytics

- o Parallel **MapReduce** leveraging hashing/distributed sorts for scalable computations.

- o **DP** for machine learning tasks (like dynamic sequence alignment in NLP or time-series predictions).

2. Case Studies of Successful Implementations (1,000 words)

2.1 Google's PageRank

- **Core Structures**: Directed Graph for websites (nodes) and hyperlinks (edges).

- **Algorithm**: Iterative approach approximating the probability of random surfers, effectively a Markov chain.

- **Complexity**: Handled billions of edges with distributed architecture, heavily optimized BFS/DFS-like computations for web crawling.

2.2 Netflix Recommender System

- **Data Structures**: Weighted Graphs or matrices representing user-item interactions.

- **Algorithms**: Collaborative filtering (matrix factorization). In practice, also uses DP-like caching and real-time priority queues for serving recommendations.

2.3 Amazon's Warehouse and Logistics

- **Data Structures**: Heaps and queues for real-time picking and packing tasks.

- **Graph Algorithms**: Pathfinding in robotic systems (like Kiva robots).

- **Optimization**: Minimizing travel time for item retrieval with BFS or Dijkstra's if environment is weighted.

2.4 Tesla Autopilot (High-Level)

- **Data Structures**: Trees for decision-making (behavior planning), tries for sensor data indexing.

- **Algorithms**: Graph-based path planning and DP for obstacle avoidance.

- **Real-Time Constraints**: Must run under strict latency. Algorithmic efficiency is paramount.

3. Final Comprehensive Project: Building a Comprehensive Application

3.1 Project Concept

We'll construct a multi-feature platform—a **"Tech Innovation Hub"**—that demonstrates how to combine multiple data structures and algorithms:

1. **User Management**: Hash tables for quick lookups of user profiles.

2. **Search and Recommendations**: Tries or BST-based systems for fast product/technology searches.

3. **Resource Scheduling**: A min-heap or priority queue for scheduling limited resources (conference rooms, dev machines).

4.   **Analytics Dashboard**: Graph-based analytics showing relationships between projects, team members.

High-Level Architecture:

- **Data Storage Layer**:

    o   users_dict (hash map) storing user profiles.

    o   resource_heap (priority queue) for resource scheduling.

    o   tech_trie for indexing technologies or projects.

- **Services**:

    o   **UserService**: Manages user add/search/update.

    o   **ResourceService**: Schedules resource usage.

    o   **SearchService**: Uses tech_trie for partial keyword matches.

    o   **GraphService**: Maintains adjacency list for collaboration analytics (team leads, projects).

- **Front-End**: (Optional) Could be a CLI or simple web UI hooking into these data structures.

3.2 Outline of Key Modules

1.   **UserService**

    o   Implementation:

python

```python
class UserService:
    def __init__(self):
        self.users = {}
```

```python
def add_user(self, user_id, data):

    self.users[user_id] = data


def search_user(self, user_id):

    return self.users.get(user_id)
```

        o   Complexity: Insertion and search are $O(1)O(1)O(1)$ on average.

    2.   **ResourceService** (Using a Min-Heap or Priority Queue)

        o   Implementation:

python

```python
import heapq


class ResourceService:

    def __init__(self):

        self.resource_queue = []


    def schedule_resource(self, user_id, priority):

        # Lower priority number => higher importance

        heapq.heappush(self.resource_queue, (priority, user_id))


    def allocate_resource(self):

        if not self.resource_queue:

            return None

        # Pop the user with highest priority (lowest priority value)
```

```python
        return heapq.heappop(self.resource_queue)
```

- o   Complexity: Insert and pop at $O(\log n)$.

3. **SearchService** (Using a Trie)

- o   Manages a trie for technology keywords or project names:

python

```python
class TrieNode:
    def __init__(self):
        self.children = {}
        self.is_end = False


class Trie:
    def __init__(self):
        self.root = TrieNode()


    def insert(self, word):
        current = self.root
        for char in word:
            if char not in current.children:
                current.children[char] = TrieNode()
            current = current.children[char]
        current.is_end = True


    def starts_with(self, prefix):
```

```python
        current = self.root

        for char in prefix:

            if char not in current.children:

                return False

            current = current.children[char]

        return True


class SearchService:

    def __init__(self):

        self.trie = Trie()


    def add_term(self, term):

        self.trie.insert(term.lower())


    def prefix_search(self, prefix):

        # Return True/False or possibly gather all terms with that prefix

        return self.trie.starts_with(prefix.lower())
```

- o Complexity: Insert or check prefix in $O(m)O(m)O(m)$, where mmm is length of the string.

4. **GraphService** (Adjacency List for Collaboration)

- o Implementation:

python


```python
from collections import defaultdict
```

```python
class GraphService:

    def __init__(self):

        self.adj_list = defaultdict(list)


    def add_relationship(self, a, b):

        self.adj_list[a].append(b)

        self.adj_list[b].append(a)  # undirected


    def find_connections(self, node):

        return self.adj_list[node]
```

- o BFS or DFS can be used to find connected components or shortest paths.

3.3 Integrating Services

Create a console-based or simple Python script that orchestrates these modules. Users can:

- **Add new user** data.

- **Request resource** scheduling.

- **Insert or search technology terms** with prefix queries.

- **Add relationships** in the graph to represent project collaborations.

- **Visualize** or list connections for a given user or project.

3.4 Testing and Validation

- **Unit Tests**: Check each service's functionality independently.

- **Integration Tests**: Verify combined workflows (e.g., user scheduling resources, searching for a project name, etc.).

- **Performance**: For large inputs (thousands of users, resource requests, etc.).

4. Preparing for Technical Interviews

4.1 Common Interview Data Structures & Algorithms

1. **Arrays, Strings**: Slicing, searching, two-pointer techniques.

2. **Linked Lists**: Reversing, merging, cycle detection.

3. **Stacks, Queues**: Parentheses matching, BFS for trees/graphs.

4. **Trees, Graphs**: Traversals (DFS/BFS), shortest path, binary search tree properties.

5. **Heaps**: Priority queue usage, heapsort.

6. **Sorting & Searching**: Merge sort, quicksort, binary search.

7. **Dynamic Programming**: Knapsack, Fibonacci variants, matrix path problems.

8. **Greedy Algorithms**: Interval scheduling, Huffman coding.

9. **Hashing**: Hash maps and sets for lookups, collision resolution.

4.2 Interview Strategy

1. **Clarify** the problem: restate it in your own words, confirm inputs/outputs.

2. **Outline Approaches**: Brainstorm brute force, then optimize.

3. **Discuss Complexity**: Time and space.

4. **Edge Cases**: Always consider empty, small, or extreme input.

5. **Code**: Write clean, modular code. Add comments or short docstrings if time allows.

6. **Testing**: Mention at least a couple of test cases (simple, edge, normal) to validate.

4.3 Tips for Success

- **Practice**: Solve many coding questions on platforms like LeetCode, HackerRank.

- **Time Management**: Keep track of time; if stuck, pivot to discussing alternative solutions.

- **Communication**: Explain your reasoning clearly. Interviewers value thought process as much as correctness.

- **Post-Interview**: Request feedback, reflect on improvements.

5. Troubleshooting and Debugging

5.1 Common Bugs and Remedies

1. **IndexErrors**: Off-by-one errors in arrays, especially in sorting or BFS loops.

2. **Infinite Loops**: Missing base case in recursion, or not incrementing pointers.

3. **Data Structure Misuse**: Using a list for queue front operations can degrade performance; deque might be better.

4. **Memory Leaks**: Typically less an issue in Python, but large DP tables or recursion can cause memory strain.

5. **Concurrency**: If using threads or async code, watch for race conditions.

5.2 Debugging Techniques

1. **Print Statements**: Step-by-step logs to isolate which iteration or subproblem fails.

2. **Python Debuggers**: pdb, PyCharm/VSCode built-in debuggers to set breakpoints.

3. **Unit Testing**: Writing tests for each function can quickly reveal where logic breaks.

4. **Binary Search Debugging**: Narrow down the line of code or function where the bug appears by halving the code path.

6. Next Steps and Continuing Education

6.1 Ongoing Learning

1. **Advanced Data Structures**: Fenwick Trees, Segment Trees, Disjoint Set (Union-Find), advanced tries (Aho-Corasick).

2. **Algorithmic Paradigms**:

   o **Backtracking** (N-Queens, Sudoku).

   o **Graph** algorithms beyond BFS/DFS (e.g., max-flow, min-cut).

   o **Linear Programming** or advanced optimization.

3. **Large-Scale Systems**: Explore distributed data structures, load balancing strategies, sharding, replication.

6.2 Applying DS&A to Career Growth

- **Technical Roles**: Roles in software engineering, data science, AI, robotics rely on DS&A fundamentals.

- **Leadership**: Understanding DS&A helps you design better system architectures and mentor junior engineers.

- **R&D and Innovation**: Many breakthroughs come from new or specialized data structures/algorithms.

6.3 Additional Resources

1. **Books**:

   o *Cracking the Coding Interview* by Gayle Laakmann McDowell.

   o *Data Structures and Algorithms in Python* by Goodrich, Tamassia, Goldwasser.

2. **Online Platforms**:

   o LeetCode, HackerRank, CodeSignal for DS&A practice.

   o Coursera, edX for specialized courses (like advanced graph theory, parallel algorithms).

3. **Conferences and Competitions**:

   o Attend meetups (PyCon, local DS&A clubs).

   o Participate in hackathons or competitive programming contests.

6.4 Final Encouragement

Data Structures & Algorithms form the bedrock of efficient, high-performing applications. Mastery takes practice—keep exploring, building projects, and testing your skills on new problems. Whether you tackle real-world healthcare systems, finance engines, or cutting-edge AI, your solid grasp of DS&A will guide you to robust, scalable solutions. Embrace a lifelong learning mindset, and you'll continue to thrive in the ever-evolving tech landscape.